ACOUSTIC GU

private lessons

BLUEGRASS
GUITAR ESSENTIALS

by SCOTT NYGAARD

Editor: Jeffrey Pepper Rodgers

Cover photograph: Rory Earnshaw

Author photograph: Anne Hamersky

ISBN-13: 978-1-4234-0841-3
ISBN-10: 1-4234-0841-1

STRING LETTER PUBLISHING

EXCLUSIVELY DISTRIBUTED BY

HAL•LEONARD®
CORPORATION
7777 W. BLUEMOUND RD. P.O. BOX 13819 MILWAUKEE, WI 53213

Copyright © 2007 by String Letter Publishing
All Rights Reserved

No part of this publication may be reproduced in any form or by
any means without the prior written permission of the Publisher.

Visit Hal Leonard Online at
www.halleonard.com

In Australia Contact:
Hal Leonard Australia Pty. Ltd.
4 Lentara Court
Cheltenham, Victoria, 3192 Australia
Email: ausadmin@halleonard.com

Contents

Introduction

Introduction
Tune-Up

Bluegrass was named after Bill Monroe's band, the Blue Grass Boys, and that band's hard-driving sound literally defines bluegrass. While the guitar was confined to a rhythm role in the Blue Grass Boys, and bluegrass guitarists still spend most of their time playing rhythm, these days bluegrass guitar tends to be associated with the virtuosic solo excursions of guitarists like Tony Rice, Doc Watson, David Grier, and Bryan Sutton. Though Monroe didn't envision guitar solos in bluegrass, the original instruments in his band have provided the models for bluegrass guitarists. From the fiddle we get fiddle tunes, from the banjo comes the inspiration for crosspicking, and blues elements derive as much from Monroe's mandolin playing as from blues guitarists. With bluegrass's recent surge in visibility, due in part to things like the popularity of the movie *O Brother, Where Art Thou?* as well as contemporary bluegrass-inspired groups like Alison Krauss and Union Station or Nickel Creek, pop and folk elements have been added to Bill Monroe's original conception.

I've touched on all these aspects of contemporary bluegrass guitar in this book, beginning with lessons in all the traditional aspects—a quick primer on bluegrass rhythm guitar, then fiddle tunes, the blues, and crosspicking—before venturing into more contemporary approaches to flatpicking, including unusual chords and solo flatpicking. I've also included profiles of three inimitable bluegrass guitar pioneers: Doc Watson, Clarence White, and Norman Blake, as well as a classic tune arranged in their playing styles.

Bluegrass is an oral tradition. Most of the music has been passed on by ear and direct example, and if you want to become a bluegrass guitarist you'll need to do a lot of listening—to recordings and live performances. And while this book should give you a thorough grounding in the essential musical elements, once you get started you'll want to seek out a bluegrass training camp, otherwise known as a jam session. You can find picking sessions in all sorts of places, from local music stores to festival campgrounds. Bluegrass is a group music—Bill Monroe would have been a country singer without his band. You can have a great time working on these lessons alone in your room, but the true rewards will come when you're playing with other people. Most of the songs and tunes in this book will be familiar to bluegrass devotees, so get out there and start picking!

Need help with the songs in this book? Ask a question in our free, on-line support forum in the Guitar Talk section of www.acousticguitar.com.

Music Notation Key

The music in this book is written in standard notation and tablature. Here's how to read it.

STANDARD NOTATION

Standard notation is written on a five-line staff. Notes are written in alphabetical order from A to G.

The duration of a note is determined by three things: the note head, stem, and flag. A whole note ( ) equals four beats. A half note ( ) is half of that: two beats. A quarter note ( ) equals one beat, an eighth note ( ) equals half of one beat, and a 16th note ( ) is a quarter beat (there are four 16th notes per beat).

The fraction (4/4, 3/4, 6/8, etc.) or ¢ character shown at the beginning of a piece of music denotes the time signature. The top number tells you how many beats are in each measure, and the bottom number indicates the rhythmic value of each beat (4 equals a quarter note, 8 equals an eighth note, 16 equals a 16th note, and 2 equals a half note). The most common time signature is 4/4, which signifies four quarter notes per measure and is sometimes designated with the symbol ¢ (for common time). The symbol ¢ stands for cut time (2/2). Most songs are either in 4/4 or 3/4.

TABLATURE

In tablature, the six horizontal lines represent the six strings of the guitar, with the first string on the top and sixth on the bottom. The numbers refer to fret numbers on a given string. The notation and tablature in this book are designed to be used in tandem—refer to the notation to get the rhythmic information and note durations, and refer to the tablature to get the exact locations of the notes on the guitar fingerboard.

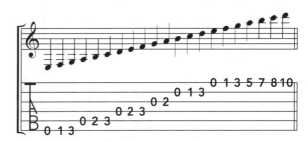

FINGERINGS

Fingerings are indicated with small numbers and letters in the notation. Fretting-hand fingering is indicated with 1 for the index finger, 2 the middle, 3 the ring, 4 the fourth finger, and *T* the thumb. Picking-hand fingering is indicated by *i* for the index finger, *m* the middle, *a* the ring, *c* the fourth finger, and *p* the thumb. Remember that the fingerings indicated are only suggestions; if you find a different way that works better for you, use it.

CHORD DIAGRAMS

Chord diagrams show where the fingers go on the fingerboard. Frets are shown horizontally, and the thick top line represents the nut. The sixth (lowest-pitched) string is on the far left, and first (highest-pitched) string is on the far right. Dots show where the fingers go, and the numbers above the diagram tell you which fretting-hand fingers to use: 1 for the index finger, 2 the middle, 3 the ring, 4 the fourth finger, and *T* the thumb. An *X* indicates a string that should be muted or not played; 0 indicates an open string.

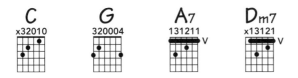

CAPOS

If a capo is used, a Roman numeral indicates the fret where the capo should be placed. The standard notation and tablature is written as if the capo were the nut of the guitar. For instance, a tune capoed anywhere up the neck and played using key-of-G chord shapes and fingerings will be written in the key of G. Likewise, open strings held down by the capo are written as open strings.

TUNINGS

Alternate guitar tunings are given from the lowest (sixth) string to the highest (first) string. For instance, D A D G B E indicates standard tuning with the bottom string dropped to D. Standard notation for songs in alternate tunings always reflects the actual pitches of the notes. Arrows underneath tuning notes indicate strings that are altered from standard tuning and whether they are tuned up or down.

VOCAL TUNES

Vocal tunes are sometimes written with a fully tabbed-out introduction and a vocal melody with chord diagrams for the rest of the piece. The tab intro is usually your indication of which strum or fingerpicking pattern to use in the rest of the piece. The melody with lyrics underneath is the melody sung by the vocalist. Occasionally smaller notes are written with the melody to indicate the harmony part sung by another vocalist. These are not to be confused with cue notes, which are small notes that indicate melodies that vary when a section is repeated. Listen to a recording of the piece to get a feel for the guitar accompaniment and to hear the singing if you aren't skilled at reading vocal melodies.

ARTICULATIONS

There are a number of ways you can articulate a note on the guitar. Notes connected with slurs (not to be confused with ties) in the tablature or standard notation are articulated with either a hammer-on, pull-off, or slide. Lower notes slurred to higher notes are played as hammer-ons; higher notes slurred to lower notes are played as pull-offs. While it's usually obvious that slurred notes are played as hammer-ons or pull-offs, an *H* or *P* is included above the tablature as an extra reminder.

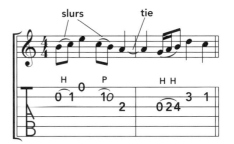

Slides are represented with a dash, and an *S* is included above the tab. A dash preceding a note represents a slide into the note from an indefinite point in the direction of the slide; a dash following a note indicates a slide off of the note to an indefinite point in the direction of the slide. For two slurred notes connected with a slide, you should pick the first note and then slide into the second.

Bends are represented with upward curves, as shown in the next example. Most bends have a specific destination pitch—the number above the bend symbol shows how much the bend raises the string's pitch: $\frac{1}{4}$ for a slight bend, $\frac{1}{2}$ for a half step, 1 for a whole step.

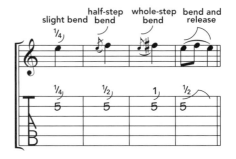

Grace notes are represented by small notes with a dash through the stem in standard notation and with small numbers in the tab. A grace note is a very quick ornament leading into a note, most commonly executed as a hammer-on, pull-off, or slide. In the following example, pluck the note at the fifth fret on the beat, then quickly hammer onto the seventh fret. The second example is executed as a quick pull-off from the second fret to the open string. In the third example, both notes at the fifth fret are played simultaneously (even though it appears that the fifth fret, fourth string, is to be played by itself), then the seventh fret, fourth string, is quickly hammered.

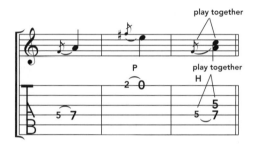

HARMONICS

Harmonics are represented by diamond-shaped notes in the standard notation and a small dot next to the tablature numbers. natural harmonics are indicated with the text "Harmonics" or "Harm." above the tablature. Harmonics articulated with the right hand (often called artificial harmonics) include the text "R.H. Harmonics" or R.H. Harm." above the tab. Right-hand harmonics are executed by lightly touching the harmonic note (usually 12 frets above the open string or fretted note) with the right-hand index finger and plucking the string with the thumb or ring finger or pick. For extended phrases played with right-hand harmonics, the fretted notes are shown in the tab along with instructions to touch the harmonics 12 fret above the notes.

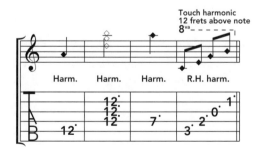

REPEATS

One of the most confusing parts of a musical score can be the navigation symbols, such as repeats, *D.S. al Coda, D.C. al Fine, To Coda,* etc.

Repeat symbols are placed at the beginning and end of the passage to be repeated.

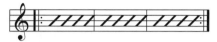

You should ignore repeat symbols with the dots on the right side the first time you encounter them; when you come to a repeat symbol with dots on the left side, jump back to the previous repeat symbol facing the opposite direction (if there is no previous symbol, go to the beginning of the piece). The next time you come to the repeat symbol, ignore it and keep going unless it includes instructions such as "Repeat three times."

Often a section will often have a different ending after each repeat. The example below includes a first and a second ending. Play until you hit the repeat symbol, jump back to the previous repeat symbol and play until you reach the bracketed first ending, skip the measures under the bracket and jump immediately to the second ending, and then continue.

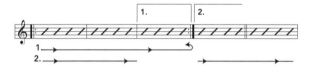

D.S. stands for *dal segno* or "from the sign." When you encounter this indication, jump immediately to the sign (𝄋). *D.S.* is usually accompanied by *al Fine* or *al Coda. Fine* indicates the end of a piece. A coda is a final passage near the end of a piece and is indicated with ⊕. *D.S. al Coda* simply tells you to jump back to the sign and continue on until you are instructed to jump to the coda, indicated with *To Coda* ⊕.

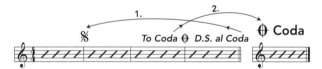

D.C. stands for *da capo* or "from the beginning." Jump to the top of the piece when you encounter this indication.

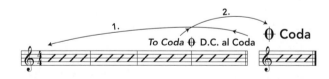

D.C. al Fine tells you to jump to the beginning of a tune and continue until you encounter the *Fine* indicating the end of the piece (ignore the *Fine* the first time through).

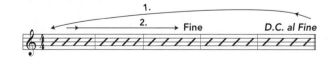

Bass Runs

At the heart of bluegrass and country guitar is the boom-chuck rhythm pattern. Here's an example in the key of G.

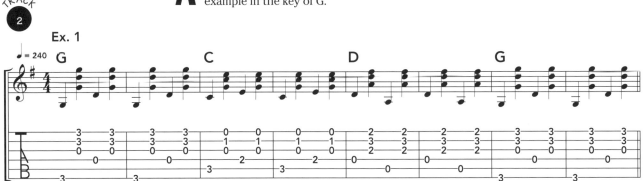

Once you've settled into this basic strum, you're bound to start looking for something else to do with your fingers—not just to stave off your own boredom but to help drive the music along and embellish different parts of a song. One easy way to do this is to add bass runs between chords. Bass runs give the music forward motion, propelling you and your band neatly into the next chord.

The most well-known bass run is the bluegrass "G-run" (Example 2), which serves more as punctuation than propulsion.

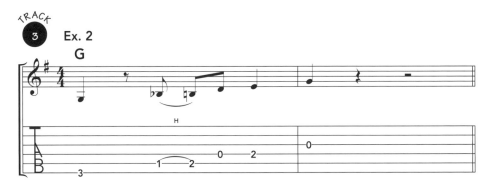

Just as a period tells you that you've come to the end of a sentence, the G-run, which usually occurs at the end of a phrase or verse of a song, signals the end of a musical thought. In this lesson, however, we'll concentrate on bass runs that continue and expand on those musical thoughts.

KNOW WHERE YOU'RE GOING

Example 3 shows one of the most common bass runs in the key of G—a simple walk-up to the C chord, using the first four notes of the G-major scale: G, A, B, C.

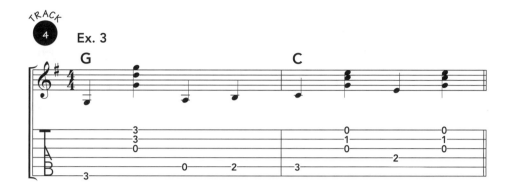

If you use your middle finger for the B note, your hand will be in a good position for the C chord. Example 4 shows a similar bass run but this time from the G to the D chord.

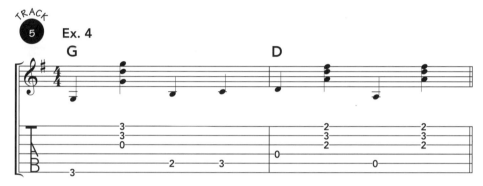

Notice that this run skips the first note of the scale, moving right to B and then C to get to the D note (the root of the D chord) at the beginning of the next measure.

This brings up one of the most important things to remember when playing or inventing bass runs: make sure you know where you're going and when you need to get there. For example, play the two G–D bass runs in Examples 5 and 6:

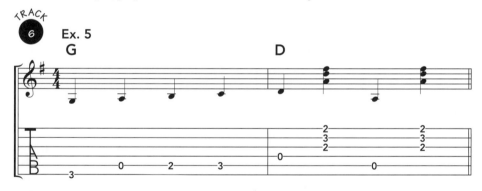

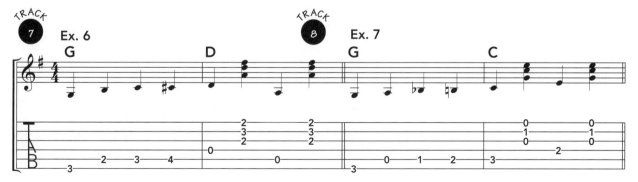

In Example 5, the run starts on the second beat of the measure rather than the third, as in Example 4. The second beat is a perfectly good time to start, but you'll notice that you have to add a note: instead of skipping the A note in the scale, you run right up the G scale to D: G, A, B, C, D.

Now imagine that you had this rhythmic idea in mind when you started your run, but instead of starting on A, you started on B, as in Example 4. To get to the D chord at the right time, you might insert a C♯ note between C and D (Example 6). Otherwise you'd get to the D chord a beat early, potentially throwing off your rhythm and eliciting malevolent glares from your fellow band members.

This inserted chromatic note (a note not in the major scale) not only saves embarrassment but also really telegraphs where you're going. The C♯ leads into the D much more emphatically than a C♮ does. Of course, it's a slightly different sound. Whether you prefer this run or the one in Example 5 is a matter of personal taste and the sound you want to add to the song. While we're at it, let's go back to the G–C change and try a chromatic run (Example 7). This time you insert a B♭ between the A and B notes to get to the C chord at the right time.

DON'T GET IN THE WAY

These chromatic notes definitely add a different flavor to the bright G-major sound, don't they? And thus we come to the next most important thing to consider: make sure your runs work with what the other musicians or singers you're playing with are doing. For example, if another guitarist is playing a simple G-chord boom-chuck pattern, alternating between G and B bass notes, that B♭ note you played in Example 7 will occur at the same time he's playing a B note: crash!

It's also important to make sure your bass notes don't get in the way of the singer's phrasing. If the melody of the song occurs at the same time you'd naturally play a bass run, it may be better to hold off on your bass runs. Some singers may not mind bass runs played while they're singing, but others may feel that a bass run hampers their freedom to phrase the melody the way they want. To keep singers happy, try a sort of walking bass (Example 8) that will stay out of their way, then put in all your fancy bass runs during the instrumental breaks.

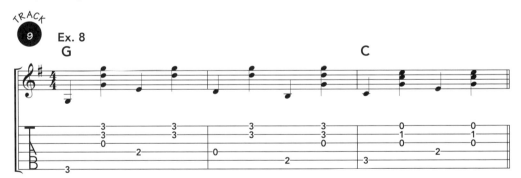

VARY THE TIMING

So far, all of these bass runs have used quarter notes played with downstrokes. But once you become comfortable with these, you might want to try a few more complicated runs using eighth notes and alternating picking—in which the primary beats are played with downstrokes of the pick and the *ands* of the beats are played with upstrokes. Example 9 is a nice run to play when you're hanging out on a D chord for a couple of measures, while Example 10 is a good way to get from D back to G.

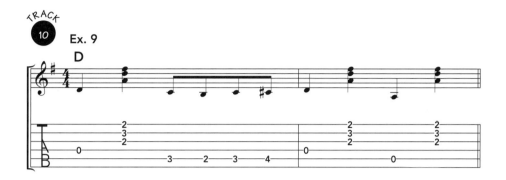

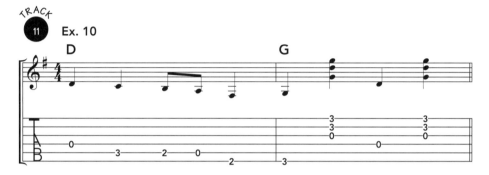

I've used most of these bass runs, plus a few others, in the accompaniment to the song "Greenback Dollar," a variant of the bluegrass standard "East Virginia Blues." The first time through, behind the vocal, takes awhile to get going, with a walking bass in the beginning and then a few more runs as you settle in. I've included more runs than you'd usually play in one verse or chorus, but you get the idea. The second time through shows the accompaniment for a simple lead guitar part (the top staff) and is a little more active. Try to get a friend to sing the words and/or play the lead guitar part so you can see how the runs work with the other parts. Then mix them up in any way you like and invent some of your own.

REST STROKES

The rest stroke is a technique used in classical music, in which your pick (or picking-hand finger if you're fingerpicking) rests on the lower adjacent string after striking the string above it. While some guitarists prefer a sort of bouncing motion with their hand when they play bass runs, the rest stroke allows you to make each note in the bass run clear and strong. It also keeps you from muddying the waters by accidentally hitting two strings.

You can try the rest stroke on any of the quarter-note bass runs in the examples, but I'll walk you through the run in Example 6 on page 9. Hit the first G note (sixth string) with a downstroke and instead of lifting your pick up in the air, let it rest on the fifth string, which will effectively mute it. You shouldn't hear any sound from the fifth string. The only sound you should hear is that nice big G note on the sixth string. This may come naturally to some, but for others it will take practice.

Once you've got the rest stroke down for the G note, lift your pick and play the B note on the fifth string, this time letting your pick rest on the fourth string. Then proceed with the C, C#, and D notes, playing a rest stroke each time. After you play the D note (fourth string), your pick will rest on the third string, where it's ready to strum the three-note D chord that follows.

Greenback Dollar

Traditional, arranged by Scott Nygaard

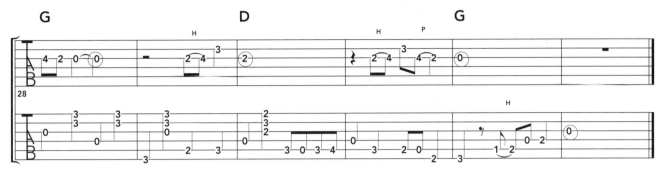

Chorus

G	**G**
I don't want your greenback dollar	2. Some folks say you love another
C **G**	**C** **G**
I don't want your watch and chain	And you care no more for me
C **G**	**C** **G**
All I want is you my darlin'	All I want is your love darlin'
D **G**	**D** **G**
Say you'll take me back again	Say you'll take me back again
G	**G**
1. Papa says we cannot marry	3. Many an hour with you I've rambled
C **G**	**C** **G**
Mama says it never will be	Down beside the deep blue sea
C **G**	**C** **G**
All I want is your love darlin'	If in your heart, you love another
D **G**	**D** **G**
Won't you run away with me?	In my grave I'd rather be

Fiddle Tunes

Fiddle tunes are the heart of old-time and bluegrass instrumental music. The lead instrument in most square dance and old-time bands, the fiddle was also essential to Bill Monroe's hypercharged old-time music long before he heard Earl Scruggs' revolutionary banjo style.

Fiddle tunes are not only great fun to play, as evidenced by their popularity at festival jam sessions worldwide, they are also great exercises in basic alternating picking, a technique that must be mastered to play fluid leads in many styles of music. The simple structure and steady stream of eighth notes in fiddle tunes allows you to concentrate on developing a smooth, even picking motion that will soon become second nature.

The concept of alternating picking is pretty easy to grasp, but the technique can be devilishly difficult to execute, especially for those players who haven't paid much attention to what their pick is doing. Basically, it's a matter of strictly alternating up- and downstrokes so that in 4/4 time, in which a measure of eighth notes gets counted *one-and two-and three-and four-and*, you play downstrokes on all the beats (*one two three four*) and upstrokes on all the *ands*. To give this a try, play through Example 1—a steady stream of open G notes.

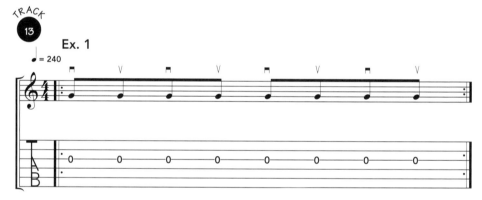

Try tapping your foot on the beats as you play through the example. If you look down at your foot and pick, you can almost imagine a string tied from your foot to your pick—the pick moving up and down in concert with your foot. Pretty straightforward, huh?

Now let's start putting some melodies to your pick strokes. Example 2 is a common fiddle tune phrase, played entirely on the G string.

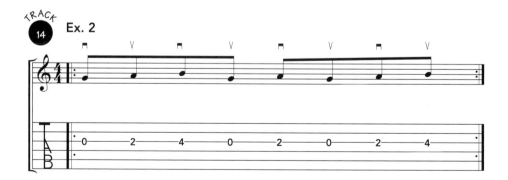

It should be pretty easy to keep your pick alternating evenly on this one, but repeat it while watching your picking hand to make sure your downstrokes and upstrokes stay on the down- and upbeats. It's natural to watch your fretting hand to make sure your fingers are in the right place, but to work on your picking, you'll have to get used to directing your gaze down toward your soundhole—especially when you start playing melodies that move from one string to another.

Example 3 is a simple run up the G scale from G to D.

Notice that the A note, played with an upstroke, is followed by a B note, played with a downstroke on a higher string, which means that your pick will have to travel a little farther to get to that open B string than if it were just going back to the G string. This shouldn't be a problem but may take a little practice. Just play it slowly, making sure you stay in time. A metronome can help here.

In Example 4 you also move from a lower string (the D note, played with a downstroke) to a higher string (the open E string, played with an upstroke).

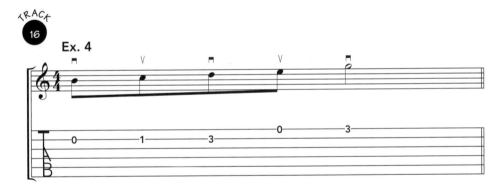

This move is easier, because after that downstroke your pick is right by the E string, poised for another stroke. But strangely, this move tends to cause more problems than the previous, more difficult move. When following a downstroke with a note on a higher string, it's natural and all-too-common to simply drag your pick across the string and play another downstroke. But if you do so and then follow that errant downstroke with an upstroke, all of a sudden you've got everything backward—you're playing upstrokes on the downbeats and downstrokes on the upbeats. This may not sound like the end of the world, but it does strange things to the rhythm of your playing—things just won't sound right until you find a way back to the correct strokes.

Examples 5 and 6 show what happens when your pick moves from a higher string to a lower one.

In Example 5, the first G note (a downstroke) is followed by a D note below it with an upstroke. Once again, your pick will have to travel a long way to get to that string. This is perhaps the hardest pick move of all, sometimes called *backpicking*. It just takes practice and attention to get right. In Example 6, an upstroke on an A note is followed by a downstroke on the D note below it, an easy move, because after an upstroke your pick is there, ready to play that lower string. And unlike in Example 4, few people tend to want to string two upstrokes together.

So, there are the four ways you move from string to string: two that are somewhat difficult, but mostly just take practice to master, and two that are relatively easy.

Besides paying attention to what your pick is doing, what else can you do to ensure smooth picking movement? The way your picking arm and hand move should be the same when you're strumming chords—playing rhythm—as when you're playing single-note leads or bass runs. If you have a nice and smooth up-and-down strumming motion, you should be able to transfer this to the way you play single-note leads. Play Example 1 and follow it with a measure of strumming on a G chord. Does your hand feel different? Is it moving in the same way in both sections? As for the best way to hold your pick and move your hand and arm, well, there is no best way. Take a handful of great flatpickers and chances are that they'll all do things slightly, or even dramatically, different. But it is important to minimize movement; wild flailing will make it harder to play cleanly. And pay attention to the angle at which your pick attacks the strings. This will have a big effect on tone, and experimenting with different angles is one way you can improve your tone. You don't want your pick changing angles much between the upstrokes and downstrokes. The best thing is for the plane of your pick to stay roughly perpendicular to the plane of your guitar's top.

OK, back to fiddle tunes. There's another thing that can throw off your pick direction: slurs, otherwise known as hammer-ons, pull-offs, and slides. Play through Examples 7 and 8 and notice that the slur takes the place of a pick stroke.

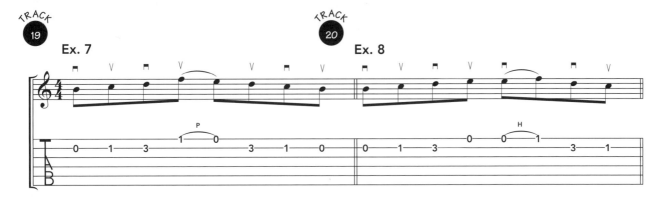

To maintain the right pick direction, you'll have to follow the missing pick stroke with the correct stroke. If the slur takes the place of a downstroke, as in Example 7, you'll follow it with an upstroke. And if the slur takes the place of an upstroke, as in Example 8, follow it with a downstroke. One way to ensure you get this right is to actually move your pick above the strings as you play the slur.

Before you have a go at the fiddle standard "Paddy on the Turnpike" on page 19, play through the G Mixolydian scale in Example 9, which contains most of the notes you'll play in "Paddy." G Mixo-what? That's just a theory-nerd way of saying "a G scale with an F♮ instead of an F♯," which can also be thought of as a C scale starting on a G note and ending on a G note. This kind of scale is sometimes called modal and has a haunting, lonesome sound.

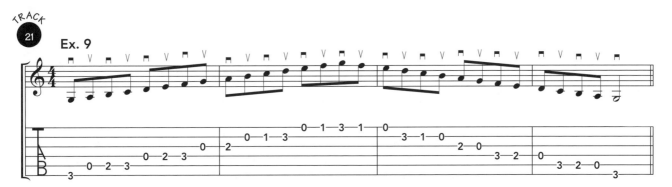

Now that I've told you how important it is to pay attention to pick direction, don't think about it too much when you're learning the melody of "Paddy on the Turnpike." It's difficult and frustrating to try to do too many things at once, and it will be a lot easier to concentrate on your pick once you've stopped trying to remember which note comes next. After you become familiar with the tune, pay close attention to all the string changes and slurs we've talked about.

But why stop at one fiddle tune? You've got the bug now, right? Give "Cuckoo's Nest" on page 20 a try. "Cuckoo's Nest" uses a lot of arpeggios, so once you've had a run through the tune, you might want to go back and practice a few of the arpeggiated passages in Examples 10–12, paying close attention to the pick direction indicated above the tab.

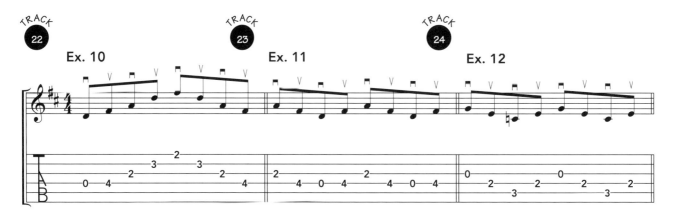

It's all strict alternating up-and-down picking but with a lot of string changes; arpeggios generally take a little more attention than some of the more scalar passages in "Paddy on the Turnpike." "Cuckoo's Nest" also contains some cool slides that mimic a common fiddle technique—sliding into the same note as an open string on the string below the open string, as shown in Examples 13–15.

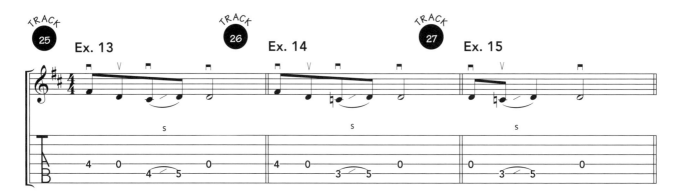

There are literally thousands of other fiddle tunes to try once you've got these nailed. As for which ones to learn next, try taking a few mental notes at the next bluegrass jam session you attend. Different groups of people have their own favorites, and it's always good to learn a tune you can play with other people. This is dance music after all, and while there's nothing wrong with dancing alone in your room, it's much more fun with a partner or two.

Paddy on the Turnpike

Traditional, arranged by Scott Nygaard

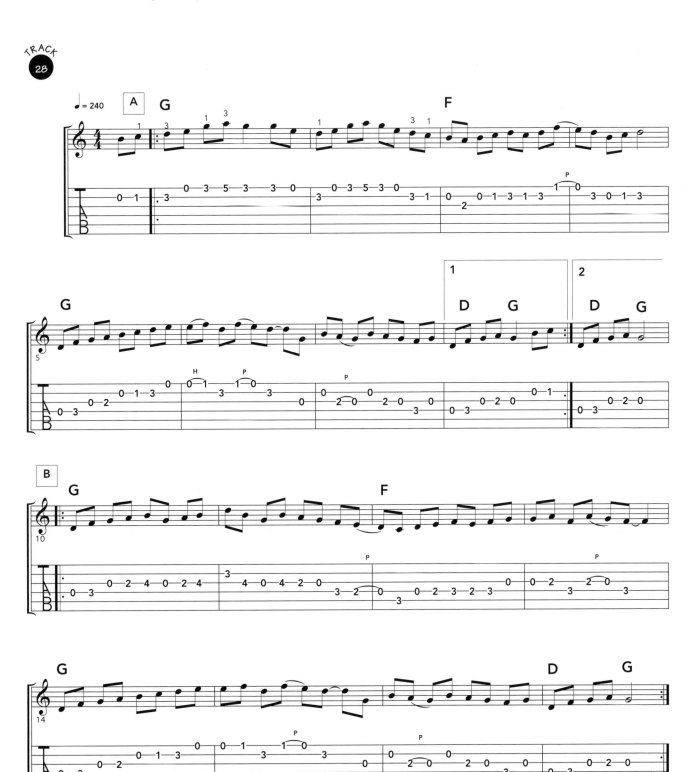

Cuckoo's Nest

Traditional, arranged by Scott Nygaard

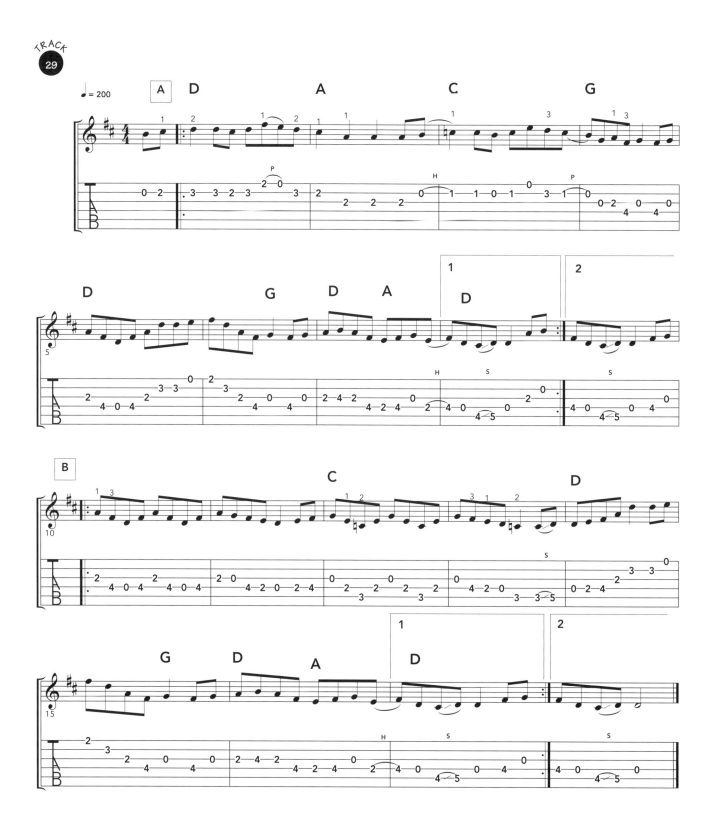

Bluesy Bluegrass

Bill Monroe played with blues guitarist/fiddler Arnold Schultz as a young man, and Schultz' bluesy influence on Monroe's music is what put the lonesome in "high and lonesome." Influenced by Monroe and others, many bluegrass guitarists—Tony Rice, Hot Rize's Charles Sawtelle, Union Station's Ron Block, Larry Sparks, and others—have made the blues an essential element of their soloing style. But playing the blues bluegrass-style—on acoustic guitars with high action and medium-gauge strings—is quite different from playing electric blues, in which the slinky strings and overdriven amps help create sustained notes and vocal effects. In bluegrass, playing the blues is more a matter of note choices and articulation, although if you develop a strong fretting hand, you should be able to slip in a bent note or two. In this lesson we'll start with a few bluesy bass runs, look at a few ways to play "blue notes," and then learn the traditional "Sugar Baby Blues."

We'll play "Sugar Baby Blues" in the key of D, but since bluegrass is so often played in G, let's start with a bluesy variation on the standard G-run (Example 1).

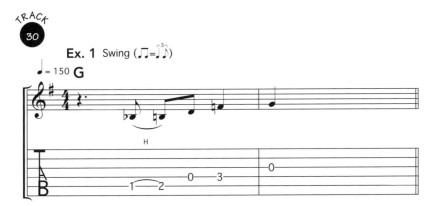

This run includes two blue notes (B♭ and F♮) that are not in the G-major scale. Unlike the basic blues approach to lead, based on the minor-pentatonic scale, bluegrass guitarists add blue notes to the major scale, sometimes using both the major third (in this case B♮) and the flatted blue third (B♭). Example 2 reverses the first G-run, starting on the open G string.

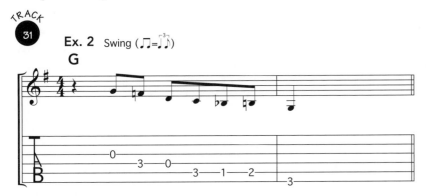

Both of these would make great fills in a medium-tempo bluesy bluegrass song. But how do you know when to use a bluesy fill and when to stick to the major scale? Simple. Listen to the singer. If she's singing blue notes, follow her example.

The lick in Example 2 also works great when transposed to D (Example 3), a great key for bluegrass blues. Slide from the F♮ to F♯ on the D string with your ring finger.

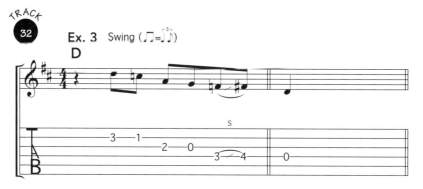

Examples 4–6 are just a few variations on this kind of one-measure fill.

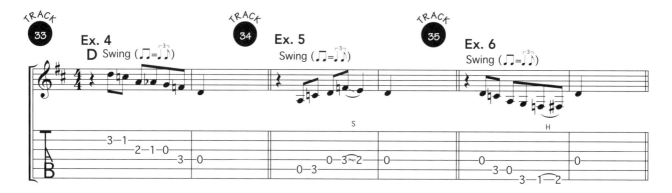

Example 4 uses another blue note: the flatted fifth (in this case A♭). In Examples 4 and 5 the flatted third is played without its cousin, the major third. These runs could also be used over a Dm chord; the tension between minor and major sounds is an important part of the blues. Example 6 is almost the same as Example 3; it starts down an octave and ends where it started: on the open D (fourth) string.

Up till now we've been approximating the bent or in-between notes singers use by leading into the major third with the minor third. Example 7 does the same thing with a bend on the D string, which is usually a little easier to bend in first position than some other strings.

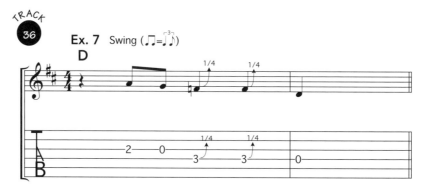

After you hit the F♮ note, either push up or pull down on the string to raise the pitch slightly. (I pull down in this case, but either way will work. Try each one to see which works best for you.) Any little bend will provide a bluesy flavor, so don't try to bend all the way up to F♯. Just push the string up a little and move to the next note. If you need extra power behind that bend, place your middle finger behind your ring finger on the third fret and use both to execute the bend.

Examples 8 and 9 also include bends, this time on the B string.

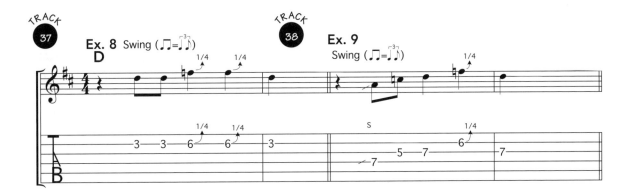

In Example 8, slide your ring finger up to the sixth fret before bending the note. In Example 9, you'll move to a higher position to bend that same F♮. Start by sliding into the A note on the seventh fret of the D string with your ring finger. This will put you in position to play the rest of the lick. Bend the F♮ with your index finger this time.

Play all these runs at a medium tempo with a bit of swing. You can use alternate picking (down-up down-up) or, to get a heavier feeling, try playing each note with a downstroke. Bill Monroe often used downstrokes on his bluesy solos, sounding a bit like Chuck Berry playing the mandolin.

Now we'll use some of these ideas in the traditional song "Sugar Baby Blues." Doc Watson called it "Honey Babe Blues" when he recorded it with Clarence Ashley and "Red Rockin' Chair" when he played it with his son Merle. It's also been called "Red Apple Juice" and other variants of these titles. This version is a bit of an amalgam of Dock Boggs' "Sugar Baby" and Watson and Ashley's "Honey Babe Blues," with a few words from West Virginia old-time banjo player Sherman Hammons.

The solo stays close to the melody both times. The first time through uses hammer-ons and the recurring F♮–F♯ lick to get the blue notes, while the second gets downright lonesome with a lot of bends. I've even added the G-run we started with way back in Example 1 as a fill on the G chord in measure 31.

The blues has always been a natural fit for guitarists, and it's no different for bluegrass guitarists. Adding a few blues to your bluegrass songbook will give you a refreshing break from those fast and furious fiddle and banjo tunes and could give you all sorts of new ideas for other tunes too.

Sugar Baby Blues

Traditional, arranged by Scott Nygaard

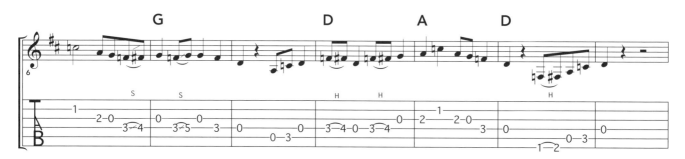

Verse

I've got no su-gar ba - by now   It's all I can do to

2—4. See additional lyrics.

keep peace with you And I can't get a - long this a way

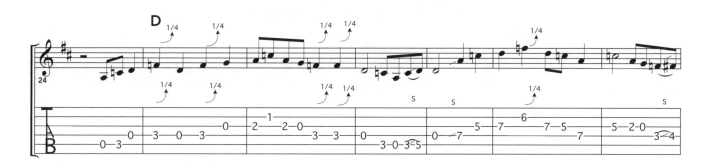

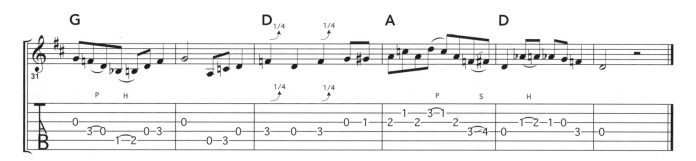

D
1. I've got no sugar baby now

         G
   It's all I can do to keep peace with you

   D   A   D
   And I can't get along this a way

D
2. Well good girl, you ain't no girl of mine

         G
   It's all I can do, it's all I can say

   D   A   D
   Gonna send you to your mama next payday

D
3. I've got no honey baby now

         G
   Some rounder come along, stole my babe and gone

       D   A   D
   And I've got no sugar baby now

D
4. I've got no honey baby now

         G
   Who'll call me honey, who'll sing this song

   D   A   D
   Who'll call me honey when you're gone

Bluegrass Kickoffs

Every solo needs a good beginning, and since the guitar is the least dynamic of the bluegrass instruments, a good kickoff is essential to every bluegrass guitarist's solo. If you're at a jam session, you don't want people skipping over you because they can't tell if you're going to play or not, and if you're playing in a band, you don't want the band thinking that the energy level is going to flag every time it's your turn to play a lead break.

A kickoff is not a particularly creative moment. It needs to be played with strength and conviction, and if it's the beginning of the song, it needs to state emphatically where the beat is. Since bluegrass solos usually follow the shape of the song's melody, most kickoffs consist of three or three-and-a-half beats that lead into one of three melody notes—the root, third, or fifth of the opening chord. Example 1 is a good solid kickoff for a song in the key of G with the melody note on the fifth (the D note). Example 2 is a similar kickoff, but the flatted seventh (F♮), flatted third (B♭), and flatted fifth (D♭) make it more appropriate for a bluesy song.

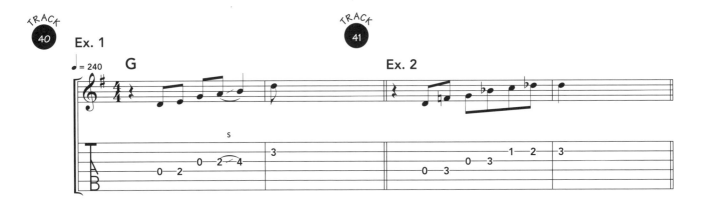

Examples 3 and 4 are kickoffs that wind up on the third of the chord, with Example 4 being the more bluesy of the two.

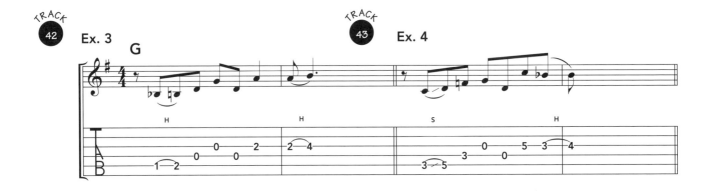

Notice that these two kickoffs start on the *and* of the first beat instead of right on beat two. All bluegrass musicians expect kickoffs to be three beats long, but anticipating the first note can give it an extra lift or swing. Make sure it's obvious where the beat is, however; you may need to accent the onbeats to make it clear.

If you really want to be certain that your bandmates know where the downbeat is, a good solid run of quarter notes like the one in Example 5 (which leads into a root melody note) is a good bet. On the other hand, if the tune has been sailing along fine without you, a flamboyant run like the one in Example 6 may be a good way to announce your arrival. Make sure you can play this one solidly before trying it, however, as a few flubbed kickoffs may leave you with fewer moments to shine when it comes time for your bandleader to hand out the solos.

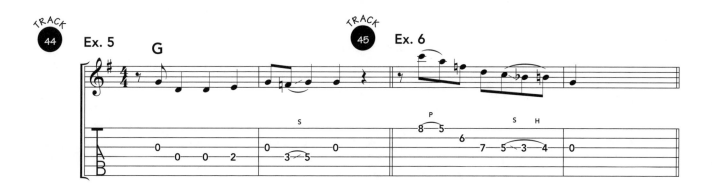

Crosspicking

Many people consider the five-string banjo to be the instrument that defines the sound of bluegrass music. Mandolinist Bill Monroe, the undisputed father of bluegrass, would probably argue the point, but when banjoist Earl Scruggs joined Monroe's Blue Grass Boys in 1946, the model for all subsequent bluegrass bands was created. The hard-driving syncopated arpeggios that give Scruggs-style banjo playing its distinctive sound are responsible for much of the fire that has led people to call bluegrass "folk music in overdrive."

It's therefore only natural that musicians who play other instruments have tried to emulate the banjo's sound. Mandolinist Jesse McReynolds was possibly the first plectrum player to try what has become known as *crosspicking*, but guitarists Bill Napier and George Shuffler, who played with the Stanley Brothers in the 1950s, were the first to adapt five-string banjo technique to the guitar to fill out the melodies of slow mountain ballads. And all the significant bluegrass lead guitarists since then have added crosspicking to their repertoire of licks and melodic devices.

The basic bluegrass crosspicking technique is achieved by playing arpeggios across three strings, dividing the eighth notes of a measure into syncopated 3-3-2 groupings. Example 1 shows the basic pattern.

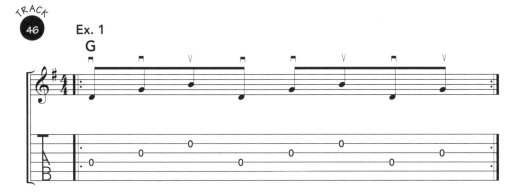

Traditionally this is played with a down-down-up, down-down-up, down-up picking pattern, which accentuates the syncopation of the roll, but it can also be played with an alternating pick direction, as in Example 2.

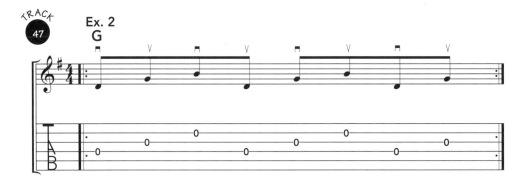

Try playing it both ways and notice how the sound changes depending on which picking pattern you use. If you're used to playing fiddle tunes and other lead lines with a strictly alternating picking pattern, you'll probably want to stick to the more familiar style, but the down-down-up pattern can be very effective.

Example 3 shows how to crosspick a melody that stays near the middle of the guitar. The melody is usually played on the lowest of the three strings, accompanied by arpeggios on the next two higher strings.

When the chords start changing, you simply change the notes of the accompanying arpeggios to match, as in Example 4.

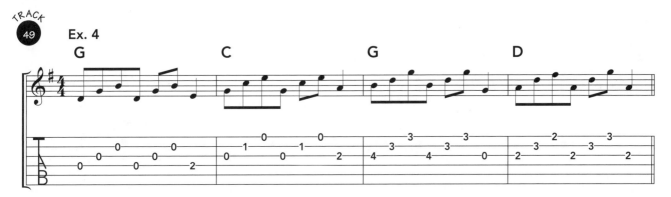

A variation on the basic 3-3-2 pattern is useful when the melody contains notes that are longer than one measure. In this case, you can simply continue the three-note rolls across the bar line, in a 3-3-3-3-2-2 pattern, often substituting quarter notes for the last two groups of eighth notes, as in Example 5.

Whether you're playing the down-down-up pattern or the alternating method, it's important to let all the strings ring into each other. You'll also need to make sure that as you change chord positions, you don't accidentally damp one of the ringing notes. Take it slowly and listen to each note to make sure it's sounding cleanly and is in time.

A metronome will help you make sure the eighth notes line up evenly. The down-down-up method may seem a bit easier at first, because you don't have to make the leap from a downstroke on a higher string to an upstroke on a lower string (the third and fourth notes in Example 2), but it can be difficult to keep those two consecutive downstrokes in the down-down-up pattern from mushing into each other, especially as the tempo increases. For that reason, I've always used the alternating method. That "backpick" may be difficult at first, but it's a good thing to get used to, because it crops up in all sorts of other places and makes the alternating version of crosspicking a great pick exercise, if nothing else.

The alternating method is essential once you start exploring other arpeggio patterns, some of which are just arpeggiated versions of strum patterns, as in Examples 6–7. And one other variation on the basic pattern, which could be called a backward roll, is handy when the melody notes move to the higher strings (Example 8).

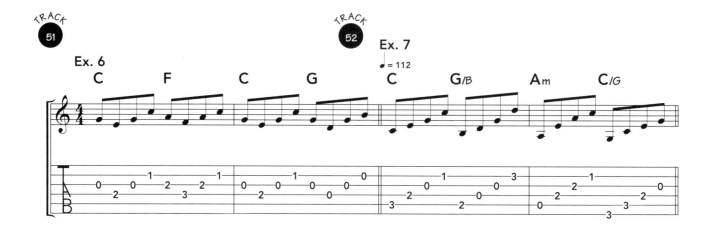

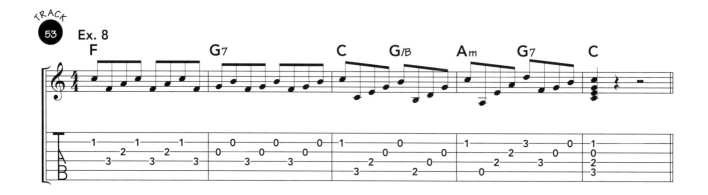

Now that we've looked at a few crosspicking patterns, it's time to use them to play the melody of a song. "Midnight on the Stormy Deep" is an old folk song first recorded by Ernest Stoneman, Irma Frost, and Eck Dunford in 1927 at the famed Bristol Sessions that launched the careers of the Carter Family and Jimmie Rodgers. It entered the bluegrass canon through Bill Monroe's version, recorded in 1966 with Monroe's son James singing lead.

Notice that the crosspicked version of the melody closely follows the sung melody notated before it. While some guitarists try to fit the melodies of the songs they're playing into the strict 3-3-2 pattern, I prefer to let the melody dictate the way I play, filling it out with a variety of crosspicking patterns and a few other kinds of runs. The guitar part begins with a short run that mirrors the melody before going into a long roll that accents the E melody note, repeating the three-note pattern four times (as in Example 5). Notice that the fourth group of three moves down a string to accent the C note, which is the melody note at that point. In measure 20 I've broken things up a bit with a different kind of run that leads into a four-note arpeggio at the beginning of measure 21. Measures 22–24 follow the melody with 3-3-2 rolls, followed by a run in measure 25 that leads into the F chord in measure 26. Since the melody has moved up to the higher strings at this point, I've used the backward roll from Example 8 and kept the three-note roll moving into measure 27. Notice the high G note in the F arpeggio in measure 27. This G is the harmony note that Bill Monroe sang on the word *her* on his recording of "Midnight on the Stormy Deep." This brief nod to the master is quickly followed by a run reminiscent of something Doc Watson or Clarence White would have played, which leads into the final crosspicked section in measures 30–31. The piece ends with the same fill we played in measure 20.

You can play the crosspicked sections here with the down-down-up picking pattern; you'll just have to switch to alternating picking when you're not playing the rolls, but this shouldn't be too difficult. Fortunately "Midnight on the Stormy Deep" is never played at a fast tempo, so you should have time to negotiate any tricky pick maneuvers. I do recommend the alternating pick style, however, as it makes it much easier to jump from one kind of run to another and allows you to insert your own licks on the fly without having to think about whether an up- or downstroke is coming next.

Midnight on the Stormy Deep

Traditional, arranged by Scott Nygaard

T'was mid-night on _____ the stor-my ___ deep _____ my so-li-ta -

2-7. See additional lyrics.

-ry watch I'd keep _____ and think of ___ her _____ I ___ left ___ be-hind ___

_____ and ask if she's _____ still true and ___ kind

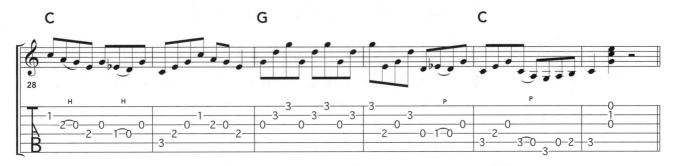

1.   C   G   C
T'was midnight on the stormy deep

My solitary watch I'd keep
                    F   C
And think of her I left behind
                    G   C
And ask if she's still true and kind

2.   C   G   C
I never shall forget the day

That I was forced to go away
                    F   C
And when I said good-bye she wept
                    G   C
And pressed me to her loving breast

3.   C   G   C
"Oh Willy, don't go back to sea

There's other girls as good as me
                    F   C
But none can love you true as I
                    G   C
Oh, don't go where the bullets fly"

4.   C   G   C
At four today a letter came

In her own hand was her sweet name
                    F   C
But then my soul filled with regret
                    G   C
As these heartbreaking words I read

5.   C   G   C
"The deep, deep sea may us divide

And I may be another's bride
                    F   C
But still my thoughts will sometimes stray
                    G   C
To thee when thou art far away"

6.   C   G   C
I never have proved false to thee

The heart I gave was true as thine
                    F   C
But you have proved untrue to me
                    G   C
I can no longer call thee mine

7.   C   G   C
So fare thee well, I'd rather make

My home upon some icy lake
                    F   C
Where the southern sun refuse to shine
                    G   C
Than to trust a love so false as thine

Going Beyond I–IV–V

If you haven't been down to your local bluegrass jam session in a while, you probably have a little catching up to do. In recent years, with modern bluegrassers like Alison Krauss having a huge influence on the scene—especially on the youngsters who are keeping bluegrass from rotting on the vine—a lot of "contemporary" songs with more adventurous harmonies and chord progressions have entered the bluegrass canon. Chord progressions that deviate from or add to the basic I, IV, V chords at the heart of bluegrass and country music have been around since Bill Monroe wrote the second part of "Rawhide" and Flatt and Scruggs recorded "Salty Dog Blues" (both of which use ragtime-era circle-of-fifths progressions), but these days you need to have a much wider harmonic vocabulary to navigate the repertoire.

You're going to have to know how to deal with B♭, E♭, Bm, E, Cm, and all sorts of other chords that may rear their pointy little heads, and you're going to have to know how to get from one to the other smoothly. Bluegrass flatpicking's fleet style relies on open strings and memorized licks to keep the lines moving along without pause. But how many B♭ licks do you know? And how many open strings are you going to be able to play over an E♭ chord? Or a Cm chord? The answer is: more than you might think.

The first thing to remember is that any of those weird chords is just a fret or two away from some chord that you are familiar with. For example, look at the Doc Watson/Clarence White–style C lick in Example 1.

Remembering that a B♭ chord is just two frets lower than a C chord, let's move that lick down two frets (Example 2).

It might not lie under your fingers quite as easily, but it's all right there. And if you fool around with it a little, you can modify it into something that won't tie your left hand in knots. Example 3 is what I came up with, but there are any number of possibilities you could find by just altering a note or two whenever you're faced with an awkward fingering.

B is between C and B♭, so if you can play that lick in B♭, you can probably come up with something similar in B. You might even add the flatted seventh to give it a B7 sound, as in Example 4.

Moving C, G, or D licks up and down a fret or two will get you to a lot of places, but you're going to end up fretting a lot more notes than you want to. So let's look at some of those weird chords and see if there are any open strings available.

Look at the E♭ and B♭ scales in Example 5.

These scales are not full major scales. They're six-note scales that skip the fourth. This scale is a good one to use when you're playing a chord progression that has gone to sea for a moment—jumped out of the main key without really modulating to another key. You could think of it as a major pentatonic scale with the seventh (or leading tone) added. But look at that—open strings! And you can play the whole scale in open position. No jumping halfway up the neck every time an E♭ chord comes around.

Now look at the G arpeggio and the B♭ arpeggio in Example 6.

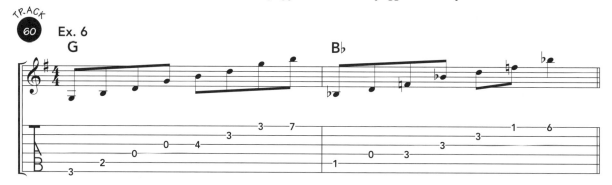

Notice how similar they look and how close some of the notes in the G arpeggio are to notes in the B♭ arpeggio. That B note in the G arpeggio is just a half step away from the B♭ note, the G note is just a whole step up from the F note in the B♭ arpeggio, and the D note in the G arpeggio is just . . . um . . . exactly the same as the D note in the B♭ arpeggio. Noting these sorts of relationships between arpeggios is the key to smoothly switching between two chords that seem to have no connection to each other. Look at Example 7 and see how smoothly the G lick moves to the B♭ lick and back again to the G lick.

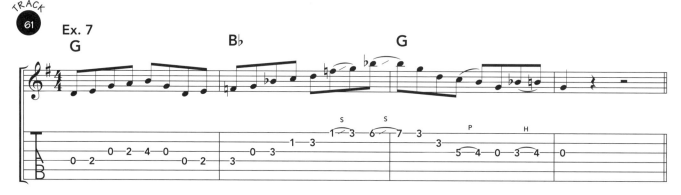

That little D–E–F line just runs right into a B♭ lick, and you can slide that high B♭ note right into a B note to get back to a G lick. Example 8 stays even closer to home—occupying the same part of the fingerboard while moving from G to B♭ and back to G.

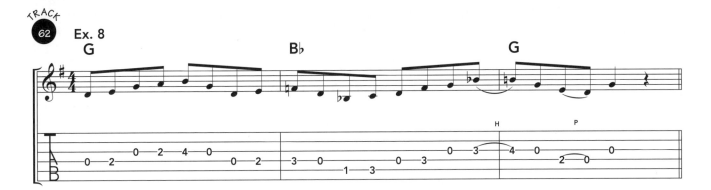

B♭ may be starting to seem like a piece of cake to you, but you've noticed I've been avoiding the E♭ chord. So try Example 9, which starts with the G lick that you're probably getting tired of and slides deftly into an E♭ run, ending neatly on a high G note.

Starting to get the idea? The thing you'll need to do when you encounter a tune that jumps around harmonically is really look at the notes of each chord you're dealing with and see how they relate to each other. "Up the Creek" on page 39 is a little tune that demonstrates how to deal with some of these chord progressions. Have a run through it, and when you're done wondering what kind of sick mind thinks this sort of thing is funny, we'll take a look at the chords I used.

The tune starts with the G–B♭ change we've already talked about. The next change is from B♭ to Em. The B♭ arpeggio, as you know, consists of B♭, D, and F, and an Em arpeggio consists of E, G, and B. Notice that the B♭ and B notes are right next to each other and that the F is just a half step away from the E. The other thing to think about when you're considering minor chords is the relative minor/major relationship. Em is the relative minor of G major, so you can use a G scale to play Em licks. Notice that measure 3 is very much like the G run we were using in earlier examples.

The next change is Em (E, G, B) to F (F, A, C). Em to F might strike you as a bit odd at first, but jumble all those notes up and add the D from the Em's natural major (G) and you've got a C-major scale. This is almost fun! Notice how I've made a smooth transition to the F chord by surrounding the C note that begins measure 4 with the B and D notes.

The next chord change is F (F, A, C) to Bm (B, D, F♯). This time I've made the transition by surrounding the F♯ of the Bm chord with an F♮ and a G. The next change is not that odd. If you remember that Bm is the natural minor of D, the Bm-to-A7 change could be like a vi–V7 change in D. But watch out for that Cm in measure 7! Let's analyze this change. A7 consists of A, C♯, E, and G, while Cm consists of C, E♭, and G. Notice that there's a G in each chord, the C is just a half step away from C♯, and E♭ is just a half step away from E. Also notice that the lick I used for Cm is kind of a modified C lick in which I've just lowered the E♮ to E♭. And speaking of E♭ (the natural major of Cm), it's just a half step above the D chord that brings the first eight bars to a close.

Make your own analysis of the chords in the second part and pay close attention to the transition points at the end and beginning of each measure: the B♭ note in measure 9 to the A note in measure 10, the B note in measure 10 to the C note in measure 11, the G note in measure 11 to the F♯ note in measure 12, the A note in measure 12 to the G note in measure 13, and so on. Every transitional phrase moves either by a half step or a whole step. Also notice that you've played this whole wacky tune in open position. It may have stretched your fingers and taxed your brain a bit, but it stayed below the fifth fret for all but one note!

Your next step is to apply these ideas to other tunes with odd chords you've run into. You probably won't find a tune that jumps around quite as often as this one. Most tunes have only one or two odd changes in them. When you practice, spend more time on those changes, and soon you'll be moving smoothly between any chords you can imagine.

Up the Creek

Traditional, arranged by Scott Nygaard

TRACK
64

New Directions in Flatpicking

The last ten to 15 years have been good ones for flatpickers. After years of holding down the rhythm in bluegrass bands, it has become de rigeur for guitarists to play as many solos as their banjo-, fiddle-, and mandolin-playing cohorts. Guitarists are now free to reinvent the role of the guitar in a bluegrass or acoustic country context, contributing whatever they want to a song, whether it's just good solid rhythm, a simple arpeggiated accompaniment, or a blistering solo. And the tried-and-true models of Tony Rice and Doc Watson have given way to more personal approaches and a variety of styles, from the blazing mandolin-inspired playing of Bryan Sutton, to the bluesy string-bending of Ron Block, to the oblique harmonies of David Rawlings. Let's take a detailed look at some of these influential flatpick-wielding guitarists and explore some of the musical ideas they've contributed.

Holding it all together is still the guitarist's job 95 percent of the time, and Del McCoury is one of the main models for aspiring bluegrass rhythm guitarists. McCoury is a master of dynamics, especially when he's backing vocals. He often barely plays behind his own singing, just hitting a few simple bass notes and strums, and then punctuates the pauses between lines with a more complicated accented strum (Example 1).

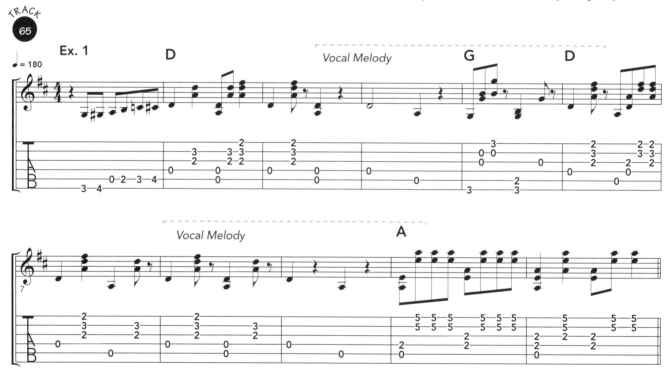

If you want to really play like McCoury, however, and you're not a vocalist, you have to stay out of the way whenever someone's mouth is open and punch the holes between vocal lines. To get the gist of McCoury's style, most people will have to make a conscious effort to play less and also to trust their bandmates to contribute to the rhythm. Flailing away as if the world would end if you missed a *boom* or a *chuck* won't cut it. While the basic bluegrass rhythm seems simple, McCoury varies it constantly, sometimes playing doubled bass notes, sometimes muting the strum or choking it off, and always varying the dynamics of each strum for the most dramatic effect.

Gillian Welch is also a minimalist rhythm master, but her style differs from McCoury's because she's usually the entire rhythm section in her duet with David Rawlings. She lays down a rhythmic mantra that won't quit until the song ends. On driving songs like "Caleb Meyer" and "Winter's Come and Gone" she gets a strong *boom chuck-a* rhythm going and adds a few bass runs and simple hammer-ons (Example 2).

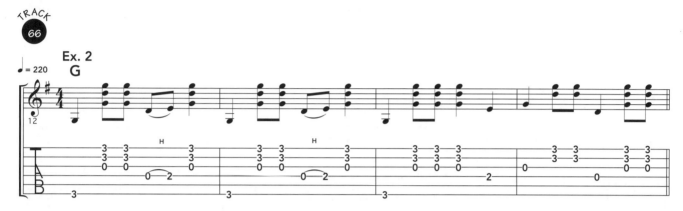

Welch's partner David Rawlings has been amazing people for years with his quirky and intense lead playing. Whereas many guitarists spend their lives trying to play the "right" notes, Rawlings consciously looks for those "wrong" notes that sound right. He loves to add notes that aren't in the chord Welch is playing, frequently playing rich sustained harmonies like those in Examples 3a–c.

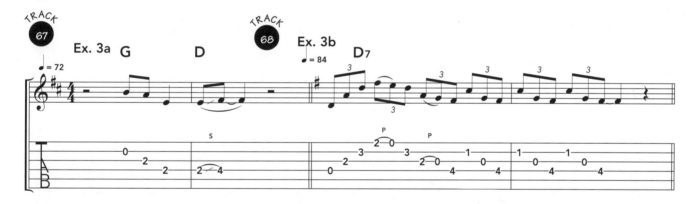

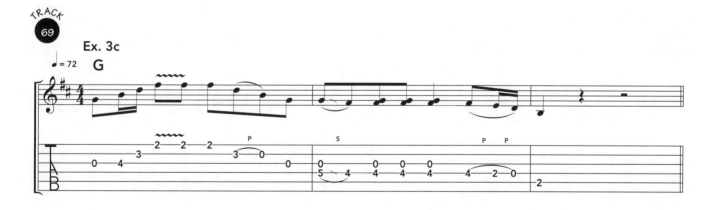

Alison Krauss' success has been a great boon to guitarists, as she's usually had two great guitarists in her band, Union Station. Her early '90s band had Jeff White on guitar and Alison Brown on guitar and banjo. She continued this two-guitar trend when Tim Stafford and Ron Block joined her band (Stafford was later replaced by Dan Tyminski). Krauss' pop ballads are often accompanied by twin crosspicked accompaniment that has become very popular among guitarists backing up slow songs (Examples 4a and 4b).

Driving the band with his five-string banjo playing is Block's primary function in Union Station, but his bluesy lead guitar playing has become an increasingly vital part of Krauss' sound. He uses bent strings and electric-style slurs to great effect (Example 5a and 5b), creating an emotional style that complements Krauss' impassioned singing.

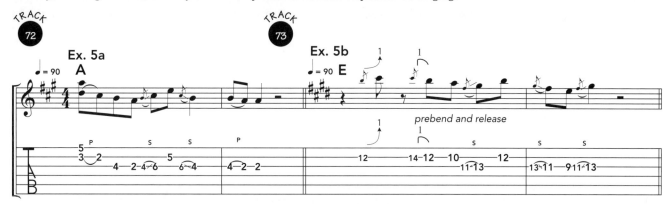

Tim Stafford has played with three great bluegrass bands (Dusty Miller, Union Station, and now Blue Highway) and has been one of the most influential rhythm guitarists of the last decade. While he can solo with the best of them, he prefers to drive the band along with powerful on-the-beat strums and syncopated accents (Examples 6a and 6b) that have redefined the traditional bluegrass band dynamics. Everyone seems to want to play rhythm guitar like Stafford. The end of the second bar in Example 6b is a typical Stafford accent. To play it right, hit the strum hard on the *and* of 3 and choke off the strum on beat 4. Then come down hard on the downbeat of the next measure with a full chord.

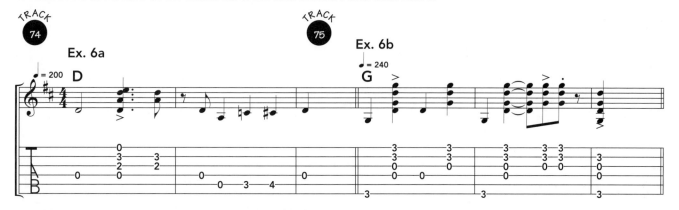

The 1990s saw the rise of some virtuosic players guaranteed to loosen the jaw. When Ricky Skaggs returned to bluegrass, the addition of North Carolina chopsmeister Bryan Sutton to his band made people sit up and take notice (and often fall out of their chairs). Sutton's playing is influenced by old-time fiddle music and the fleet chromaticism of mandolin players like Adam Steffey and Chris Thile. He can play fluid lines like the one in Example 7 at any tempo he cares to.

Another highly influential player is Kenny Smith, who first came to attention in the popular Lonesome River Band and now co-leads the Kenny and Amanda Smith Band. While Smith's powerful rhythm playing defines the modern hyperactive bluegrass rhythm style, his distinctive solos include Clarence White–like syncopated bluesy crosspicking (Example 8a) and flashy runs that make use of open strings (Example 8b). The four-fret stretch in the last measure is made a little easier by playing it in the Lonesome River Band's favored key of B (or as we guitarists call it: capo four), but it's still a fingerbuster at any tempo.

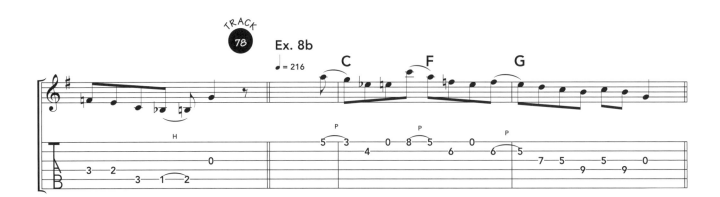

Another guitarist of note is Nickel Creek's Sean Watkins. Watkins' lead playing is influenced by the lyricism of Russ Barenberg and Ron Block, and his creative accompaniments are perfect for the complex instrumentals and pop-influenced songs that he and bandmate Chris Thile specialize in. Example 9a takes the kind of sus2 arpeggio favored by Alison Krauss and twists it into a syncopated Gordian knot, while Example 9b is a more relaxed version of the same groove.

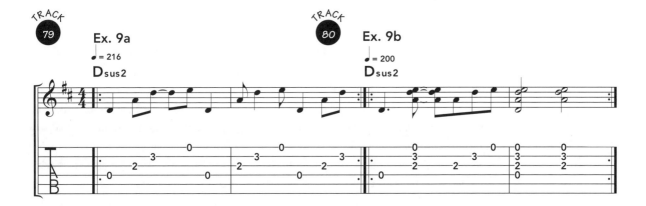

David Grier has been arguably the most creative and influential flatpicker of the last two decades. Originally inspired by the innovations of Clarence White and Tony Rice, Grier has created his own virtuosic style full of quirky rhythmic and harmonic ideas colored by his mischievous sense of humor. Like Watkins, Grier also likes to play with time, and the slippery licks in Examples 10a and 10b are the sort of thing he revels in.

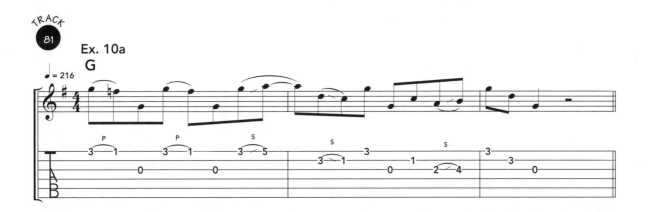

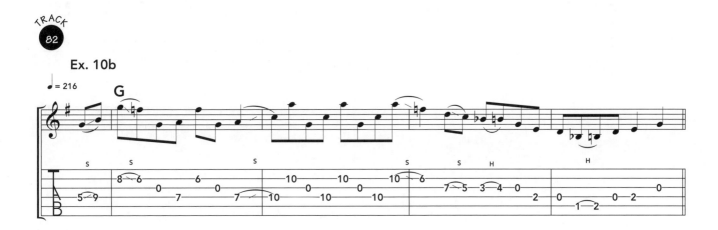

Solo Flatpicking

When people use the term flatpicking to denote a musical style, they're usually referring to the furious fiddle tunes and hot instrumentals spun out by the likes of Doc Watson, Tony Rice, and David Grier. But lead guitar in a bluegrass or old-time setting really began back in the 1920s with Maybelle Carter's melodic song-based guitar solos with the Carter Family. Carter created her self-contained sound by playing the melody to songs while accompanying herself by strumming in the keys of C or G. Although flatpicking tends to be a social sport, some players (Clarence White, Beppe Gambetta, David Grier, and others) have expanded on Carter's example by accompanying songs and fiddle tunes with open bass strings.

The preferred flatpicking keys of G, D, and C, however, don't provide much in the way of open bass strings, except for the fourth (D) string, which is really not all that low and often ends up being used as a melody note in the key of D. One easy way to get a full bass sound that will allow you to accompany yourself is by lowering your sixth string from E to D, which puts you in dropped-D tuning (D A D G B E). Most bluegrass players have shied away from open tunings, primarily because the string tension of standard tuning seems to produce the right timbre—a nice tight snap with a full rich sound. But this is a small modification, and if you use medium-gauge strings (or at least a medium sixth string), your guitar will retain most of the timbre of standard tuning, and it's also relatively easy to switch back and forth between dropped D and standard. The advantage of dropped-D tuning becomes obvious once you strum all six strings of an open D chord—finger the D as you normally would but this time add the lower strings.

This full chord sounds great and you don't have to use any left-hand fingers on the bottom three strings. This is important because you'll need your fingers to play the melodies.

GETTING STARTED

Try playing a simple D-major scale in open position (Example 1) and then slowly strumming the bass strings as you play each note of the scale (Example 2).

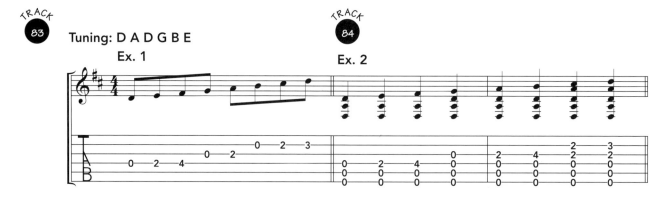

Some notes will sound better than others, but you get the idea. Now let's get a little more precise and simply play one bass note to accompany each note of the scale (Example 3).

Ex. 3

Just alternate melody and bass notes for now, sticking to the I, IV, and V chords in D (D, G, and A). Notice that you now have to fret the G bass note up on the fifth fret of the sixth string, but also notice that the two melody notes that are naturally harmonized by the G chord—the G and B notes—are both open strings. So you don't have to work too hard.

There are all sorts of melodies you can play in dropped D. The first thing you might want to do is play some tunes you already know and see if you can throw in a few bass notes while you play them. The easiest place to put them is at the beginning of the melodic phrase (or downbeat) and in places where the melody note is a quarter note or longer.

If you're confused, take a look at my arrangement of the old spiritual "Kingdom Come" on page 49. Notice how I strum the lower three strings on the downbeat of measure 1 and then alternate the melody notes (F♯s) with the low D bass note. These bass notes occur on the second and fourth beats of the measure rather than the usual first and third beats bass notes like to inhabit. This is done to get the melody notes in the right place, but it also sounds kind of cool—a little modification of standard practice. The main thing is that you're now playing melody and bass notes simultaneously and you haven't had to put any of those weird metal things on your right-hand fingers or visit a nail salon to toughen up your nails. You're doing it all with your trusty flatpick.

You'll notice as you progress with the melody of "Kingdom Come" (measures 2–4) that the bass notes become a little erratic as the melody gets more complicated. Not to worry. A relentless bass line is often not all it's cracked up to be. This is one thing that hangs flatpickers up when they try to accompany themselves in this manner. They think they've failed somehow if they're not playing a regular alternating bass. Remember, you're just trying to fill out a melody, not make surrounding jaws drop to the floor.

Things get a little tricky when you have to change to a G chord. But notice what happens in measure 5 when the G appears. Strum the chord on the downbeat (using a voicing that includes the melody notes on top) and then hit the bass note once more in a hole in the melody (beat 2) followed by another open D (sixth string) in another hole in the melody (the *and* of beat 3). Once again, it's not the way a bass player would play it, but it gives you the chord change you need. Notice the A bass note in measure 6, which provides a quick I–V–I cadence at the end of the first part.

"Kingdom Come" is constructed with a common AABA song structure, and the second time through the A part is a bit more complicated, with a few bass notes coming on the offbeats (measures 10 and 11). I'm filling in a little more now, and this might be a bit much for some players, but notice that pull-offs are used to play the melody notes before these bass notes, which gives your pick a little more time to jump back down to the sixth string.

The bridge (measures 17–22) gets a bit more complicated as the melody moves up to the top strings and there are more G bass notes to fret, so I decided to change the texture of the bridge by simply strumming a full chord on the downbeat of each measure. This is a handy arranging tip to keep in mind. A repetitive texture or rhythm can get boring, so always look to see if you can simplify the accompaniment when the melody or chord changes become more complicated.

In the last A part I've added a couple of different chord changes at the end (measures 27–28) to give the tune a little variety and a sense of closure. I've found that, when playing AABA tunes that cycle over and over, it's nice to give the third A part a different treatment than the first two. For one thing, it keeps you from getting lost in all those repeating parts.

Dropped D can be the slippery slope into the abyss of open tunings. G6 tuning (D G D G B E) is just a turn of the peg away and is a great way to accompany G tunes. And once you get started twisting your tuners, who knows what you'll find. You may also want to investigate playing some tunes in the keys of A or E in standard tuning, as the bass notes of standard tuning (E, A, and D) are perfect for those keys. Clarence White used to play a beautiful slow version of "Soldier's Joy" in the key of A using the low A string to accompany the melody. And I've become fond of playing G tunes in E, capoed at the third fret. The possibilities are endless.

Kingdom Come

Traditional, arranged by Scott Nygaard

Tuning: D A D G B E

Doc Watson

Doc Watson is a one-man folk festival. Listen to a few of his albums or one of his spellbinding performances and you're likely to hear mournful, flinty clawhammer banjo straight out of the North Carolina mountains; melodic country harmonica (imagine a blues harpist sitting in with a square-dance band); propulsive 12-string fingerpicking (a bridge between Leadbelly and Leo Kottke); mountain ballads and hymns intoned in that molasses and sunlight baritone that somehow recalls both Watson's and the listener's home and hearth; six-string fingerpicking alternately recalling Merle Travis and Mississippi John Hurt yet easily identified as Watson's own; novelty songs and classics from the dawn of recorded country music; and the clean, fast, fluid, swinging, breathtaking flatpicking that has influenced every acoustic guitarist attempting to gain control over a small, triangular piece of plastic in the last 40 years.

This last style is where Watson has been a true revolutionary, at least in the bluegrass world. While he has never identified himself as a bluegrass guitarist (if the definition of a bluegrass guitarist is a guitarist who plays in a bluegrass band, then he is correct), Watson's 1963 performance of "Black Mountain Rag" is on a par historically with Earl Scruggs joining Bill Monroe's Blue Grass Boys. While there had been some prior instances of lead guitar in a bluegrass band, most notably Don Reno and Stanley Brothers guitarists Bill Napier and George Shuffler, there had been nothing that proved how exciting and dynamic the acoustic flattop guitar could be as a solo instrument. Watson's perfectly designed minute and a half of flatpicking lit up the sky with possibility and showed the way for all who would follow. Here was the first true flatpicking instrumental, influenced by the fiddle but able to stand on its own as a guitar piece.

Oddly enough, while Watson grew up with traditional music all around him, he didn't really start trying to play fiddle tunes on the guitar with any seriousness until he was playing electric guitar in a dance band. Most of the members of the Watson family of Deep Gap, North Carolina, were conversant in traditional music and folklore—the family would sing a few hymns from a southern hymnal before bed each night—but Arthel "Doc" Watson was different; he was blind. Unable to pursue his interest in electronics as a career, Watson soaked up the traditional hymns, ballads, and dance music around him as well as the music of artists like the Carter Family, the Delmore Brothers, Riley Puckett, and Jimmie Rodgers that he heard on the radio. In 1954 Watson formed a honky-tonk band with pianist Jack Williams to play at dances in the area. "Most of the time the little group I played with didn't have a fiddler, but the people who we played with would want a square-dance set, so I'd do the fiddle tunes on the [electric] guitar," Watson explains.

Watson is a master of banjo, harmonica, mandolin, and guitar, but the fiddle remains outside his grasp. "I love the fiddle awfully good, but I couldn't get much more than a hungry pig out of it," he says, chuckling. Inspired to do so out of necessity but also from the example of Joe Maphis, Grady Martin, and Hank Garland, Watson began to learn the tunes he'd heard at home on the guitar and play them for weekly dances. "I got in a lot of technical practice in the '50s, then when the folk revival came in the early '60s I got caught up in that and turned back to the flattop," Watson recalls.

The urban folk world discovered Watson soon after Ralph Rinzler and Eugene Earle traveled to Mountain City, Tennessee, to record banjo player and ballad singer Clarence Tom Ashley. Ashley had gathered around him a number of the best musicians in the area, including Watson, and after a day spent in Deep Gap with Watson's father-in-law, fiddler Gaither Carlton, and the rest of the Watson family, Rinzler understood what a prodigious talent he had stumbled upon. Watson was soon traveling with Ashley, Carlton, Fred Price, and Clint Howard to many of the major folk venues and festivals around the country, and within a couple of years he was appearing by himself, recording his first album, *Doc Watson*, for Vanguard in 1964.

Watson also began performing with his son Merle in 1964, an association that would last until Merle's tragic death in 1985. Stunned by this loss, Doc quit touring for awhile, but decided to try to keep his son's memory alive by starting the Merle Watson Memorial Festival, now known as Merlefest. Held each April in North Wilkesboro, North Carolina, it began as a gathering of friends, a tribute to Merle from some of the best acoustic musicians in the world. "The first festival really showed how many friends Merle had. Nearly everyone that was there knew Merle and loved him for who he was, not what he'd accomplished. It's something that I and the whole family really appreciate—what the festival's done for Merle's memory," Doc says.

Since then Merlefest has become one of the most highly regarded acoustic music festivals in the world, and it reflects Watson's own musical diversity with its wide-ranging lineup.

These days, Watson performs infrequently, but his love of playing has not waned. "I play the guitar because I love it better than any other instrument that I could ever hope to learn," he's said. "When I play a song, I live that song, whether it is a happy song or a sad song. Music, as a whole, expresses many things to me—everything from beautiful scenery to the tragedies and joys of life. A good guitar is like a friend. Sometimes when you're lonely, bored, or depressed, you pick that guitar up and play and all at once it's gone."

Black Mountain Rag

Traditional, arranged by Scott Nygaard

Doc Watson learned "Black Mountain Rag" from fiddler Leslie Keith, who played it in the key of A with his fiddle cross-tuned to A E A C♯ (often called "Black Mountain Rag" tuning by old-time fiddlers), and transformed the unique fiddle piece into an equally unique guitar piece. When a fiddler plays it, the mood is very different. The open drone strings of the fiddle give it a lonesome, archaic sound. Rather than trying to imitate this quality, which would have probably proven the guitar's inferiority in evoking such a sound, Watson put the tune in the key of C, capoed to D, and reworked the melody into an exhilarating display of virtuosity. The last section in particular is enough to launch listeners from their chairs just as they're getting used to the speed and clarity of the opening sections. Every flatpicker of note has come up with his own version (this is mine), but each is indebted to Watson.

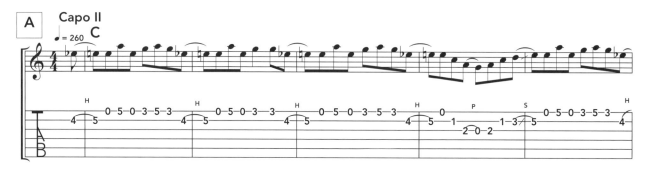

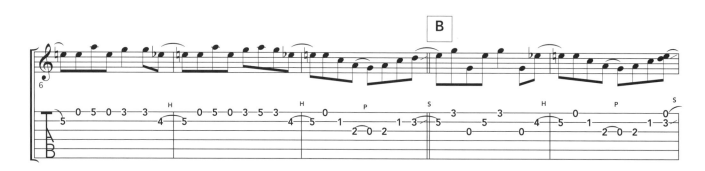

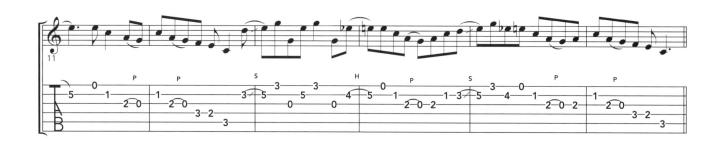

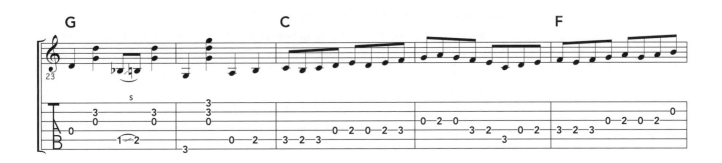

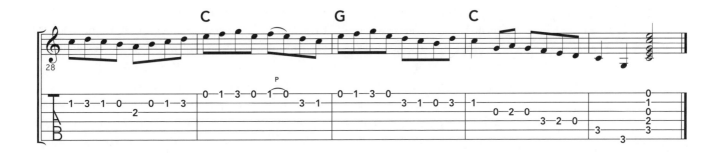

Clarence White

Most guitar innovators have restricted their efforts to either the acoustic guitar or the electric guitar, and while some have tried their hand at both instruments, their usual approach has been to simply transfer one instrument's technique and style to the other. Clarence White, however, can rightfully claim to be the only guitarist in history to have invented unique ways of playing both acoustic and electric guitar.

His electric playing, with Nashville West and the Byrds, combined elements of the influential country styles of James Burton and Joe Maphis with the slippery sounds of the pedal steel, forming the basis for contemporary country lead guitar. As a bluegrass guitarist, his solos with the Kentucky Colonels were the first to match the level of dynamism and virtuosity previously achieved by fiddle, mandolin, and banjo, while his sense of rhythm, a unique combination of rock-solid groove with a sophisticated style of syncopation, brought a feeling of freedom and exploration to a music that was just beginning to venture beyond its traditional roots. He achieved all this despite his tragic death at the age of 29.

Clarence White was born into a musical family in the small town of Madawaska, Maine, on June 7, 1944. His father, Eric Sr., played fiddle, guitar, banjo, and harmonica, and music pervaded the White household. White's father and uncles often played together around the house, and soon Clarence and his siblings, Roland, Eric Jr., and Joanne, were joining in. "Joanne and I sang from the time we were six or seven," says Roland, who is ten years older than Clarence.

"I figured out a few chords on the guitar so that we could accompany ourselves. We sang songs that we heard our father do, country music mostly, and that we heard on record. My mother had tons of 78s—country music from the '20s on up to the '50s. We had this big old console record player, and we just played those records and imitated that. My dad played fiddle—instrumentals, 'Ragtime Annie,' 'Soldier's Joy,' 'Back Up and Push,' some French-Canadian tunes that he had French titles for. We performed some—at grange halls and things, where they'd have a little entertainment for the local people—but mostly we'd go to relatives' houses on the weekend, and they'd expect us to pick and sing. My dad and his brothers, four of five of them, would play whenever there was a gathering. They'd play for everyone to dance to or they'd sing. It was anything goes—if you knew it, you sang it." Clarence began joining the throng on guitar at the age of six, giving his first performance at a local grange hall at the age of eight.

Two years later, the family moved to Burbank, California, and after winning a talent contest sponsored by a local radio station, the youngsters began performing as the Three Little Country Boys, with Clarence on guitar, Roland on mandolin, and Eric Jr. on banjo and bass. They appeared on numerous local radio and TV shows throughout southern California, including the TV show *Town Hall Party*, which also included regular appearances by country guitarist Joe Maphis, who would become a major influence and mentor, introducing Clarence to the music of Django Reinhardt and Charlie Christian and influencing the Whites' approach to performing.

Bluegrass became a dominant influence after Roland bought a copy of Bill Monroe's recording of "Pike County Breakdown" in 1956, and when five-string banjoist Billy Ray Lathum joined the group in 1958, the Country Boys were transformed into a full-fledged bluegrass band, with Leroy Mack adding his Dobro to the developing sound soon after. Records by Flatt and Scruggs, the Stanley Brothers, and Reno and Smiley became fodder for emulation, and in 1959 the Country Boys cut their own single for the Sundown label. With the folk music boom in full swing, they began performing around the L.A. area at the Ash Grove and other clubs and coffeehouses, even making a national TV appearance on the *Andy Griffith Show*.

It was around this time that Clarence began to seriously consider the guitar as a lead instrument. "I think by watching Joe Maphis and Merle Travis and those kinds of guitar players on the *Town Hall Party*, he picked out a couple things," says Roland. "But we were never serious about doing it in the band. Then I acquired a record—Reno and Smiley's 'Country Boy Rock 'n' Roll.' I liked the way they played the guitar on that, so I kind of learned it and brought it to Clarence's attention, and in no time he played it. He just knew exactly where to go with it." Clarence composed his first solo for the Stanley Brothers song "Journey's End," performing it in public for the first time at the Ash Grove on September 19, 1961 (amazingly enough, this performance was recorded by Mike Seeger and can be heard on *Living in the Past* on Sierra Records). Roger Bush took over the bass chair in 1961 when Eric Jr. married, and a planned East Coast tour was cut short by Roland's untimely conscription into the Army.

While Roland was performing his military duties, the band recorded its first LP, *New Sound of Bluegrass America*, produced by Carter and Ralph Stanley with Gordon Terry and Jelly Sanders sitting in on fiddle. The group's name was changed around this time to the Kentucky Colonels to avoid confusion with Mac Wiseman's backing group, also called the Country Boys. With Roland gone, Clarence began to solidify his evolving style. Doc Watson made his first West Coast appearance in the spring of 1962, and his virtuosic flatpicking stunned the teenager with its speed and fluidity. "Clarence heard Doc Watson play at the Ash Grove," says Roland. "And it just turned him on. He said, 'Wow. This is the way to play this kind of music.'" Under Watson's influence, Clarence began to take more solos in the band and soon realized the potential for making lead guitar a viable part of a bluegrass band. His rhythm playing also assumed a more active role, and he began interjecting flashy, syncopated bass runs that jabbed and prodded the soloists. He made his recording debut as a lead guitarist on *New Dimensions in Banjo and Bluegrass* (now available as the soundtrack to *Deliverance*) by Eric Weissberg and Marshall Brickman, and word of his prowess began to spread beyond the California border.

After Roland returned from the Army, the group recorded *Appalachian Swing*, an album of instrumentals that would become a bluegrass classic (in order to save on recording costs, the group was asked to dispense with vocals). All the elements of Clarence's style were in place at the age of 20, and the Colonels performed these traditional pieces with a preternatural cohesion. While all of the Colonels were good singers, it was their instrumental virtuosity and sophisticated sense of interplay that stood out. Clarence and Roland's guitar and mandolin weave in and out of each other so naturally that at times it is easy to become confused as to who is playing lead and who is playing backup, a kind of simultaneous soloing that was unheard of in bluegrass and has rarely been explored since.

Some of the tunes on *Appalachian Swing* were recorded with the tape running as the band was getting warmed up, then spliced together later to capture the best moments. "I don't know how many we did like that," says Roland. "But I know that we weren't getting anywhere with one of them and he [Richard Bock, who recorded the album] said, 'You guys are always better when you're into it, so just keep playing and I'll splice it all together so it makes sense. I was there one day when he was working on one of 'em. He had tapes hanging everywhere, and I thought, 'Oh, no.' I didn't know how he was going to make sense of all that, but he did."

The band's tightness also allowed the Colonels to play with an intensity that bordered on chaos. Live recordings from this period show a group of daredevils performing without a net and always managing to emerge unscathed from their wild excursions. "We got that, I think, from Dad and his brothers when they were playing," says Roland. "They'd romp and stomp on a tune. It wasn't fast, but they just got a little wild. And Joe Maphis would pull off stuff like that. He was really a showman. Even Monroe did that."

Clarence staked out his flatpicking territory on *Appalachian Swing*. Watson was known for tearing the house down with his smooth guitar versions of traditional fiddle tunes, and while Clarence could match his speed and rapid-fire attack when the situation demanded, he shone on the medium-tempo songs that allowed him to develop his radical ideas of space and timing. "We used to sit around playing tunes a lot," says Roland. "And we'd just do some syncopated runs or rhythms to try to get each other off purposely, and that kind of turns you on to ideas and makes you think. You'd think about it, and you'd say, 'I could use that.'"

Clarence's syncopated, bluesy playing on songs like "I Am a Pilgrim" and "Nine Pound Hammer" were revelations. And on the fiddle tunes "Billy in the Lowground" and "Sally Goodin," he proved that there was an alternative to Watson's smooth, old-time style of flatpicking. White's playing often eschewed the fluidity of fiddle music, with phrases that lurched into being in surprising ways. Small chordal fragments and fractured arpeggios burst from pauses in odd places, while echoes of all his influences were deftly altered to sound totally fresh. But it is White's phrasing and time that are remarkable and virtually without precedent. No bluegrass guitarist before or since has had such a sophisticated sense of time.

After the release of *Appalachian Swing*, the Colonels (with Jerry Garcia in tow) embarked on a tour of the East Coast, a tour that included a performance (captured on *Long Journey Home*) at the Newport Folk Festival. The highlights of this wonderful recording are the half-dozen impromptu guitar duets performed by White and Watson at a guitar workshop. The recordings of "Farewell Blues" and "Beaumont Rag" in particular point out the differences in the two seminal flatpickers' styles. Watson is fluid, relaxed, and (at least to today's ears) somewhat predictable, but while White's fingers occasionally stumble in the cold air of the outdoor workshop, he is wildly inventive and clearly unafraid to take chances. The delight Watson took in listening to his young protégé is evident. His cries of "Yeah, man" and "Look out, boy" punctuate the recording.

The Colonels continued to perform throughout California after their return (many of the live recordings heard on *Living in the Past, The Kentucky Colonels: 1965–1967, The Kentucky Colonels Featuring Clarence White,* and *On Stage* are from this period), but soon, as the folk scare started to subside, they found it difficult to get gigs. They were unable to secure another recording contract, and the nascent bluegrass festival circuit deemed them too progressive for their audience. The British Invasion had swept the states in 1964, Dylan had gone electric, the Byrds had recorded "Mr. Tambourine Man," and it began to look as if acoustic folk music was going to be left behind by its mod cousin, folk rock. The Colonels tried to join the electric wave, taking a regular job as an electric band playing country hits in a bowling alley, but after a show on Halloween 1965, the band dissolved.

Clarence had always been interested in music other than strictly traditional bluegrass, as evidenced by live recordings of tunes like "Sheik of Araby" (*Living in the Past*) and "When You're Smiling" (*The Kentucky Colonels Featuring Clarence White*). He had in fact been given an early demo of "Mr. Tambourine Man" by Bob Dylan when he was looking for material for a proposed but never realized solo guitar album. "Most of the guys in the [Colonels] weren't interested in doing a song like 'Tambourine Man,'" he said in an interview that appeared in *Full Circle* (Fall '84). "They were just interested in doing straight, old-time bluegrass."

White purchased a 1954 Fender Telecaster in 1965 and began the next stage of his musical development. He had been friends with James Burton, Jimmy Bryant, Don Rich, and Duane Eddy since the early '60s, and he began combining ideas from their playing with his own style. Burton was particularly influential. He was earning a comfortable living as a session guitarist, and White determined to do the same. He quickly found session work and with Gib Gilbeau and Gene Parsons formed the country-rock group Nashville West.

White didn't completely give up on the acoustic guitar or bluegrass, however. The Colonels reformed for a few months between December 1966 and May 1967, with brothers Roland and Eric on mandolin and bass, Bob Warford on banjo, and Dennis Morris on rhythm guitar. Live recordings of this band (heard on *The Kentucky Colonels: 1965–1967* and *The Kentucky Colonels Featuring Clarence White*) show White experimenting (not always successfully) with some of the ideas he was developing on the electric guitar, including bending strings and combining his flatpick with his fingers. With a rhythm guitarist in the band, he was also freer to solo whenever he wanted to. He did some of his wildest playing in this incarnation of the Colonels, which performed sporadically and dissolved again when Roland took a job as guitarist in Bill Monroe's Blue Grass Boys.

One of the sessions White played on around this time would dramatically change his life. In late 1966, longtime friend and fellow bluegrass musician Chris Hillman of the Byrds brought White into the studio to play on the songs "Time Between" and "The Girl with No Name," which were released on the folk-rock supergroup's *Younger Than Yesterday*. White would also perform as session guitarist on the next two Byrds releases, *Notorious Byrd Brothers* and *Sweetheart of the Rodeo*. The latter recording was highly influential in the development of what would become country rock. After Gram Parsons left the Byrds in the summer of 1968, White was enlisted as his replacement and stayed with the group until its dissolution in 1973.

In February 1973, White was invited to join a one-off band opening for Bill Monroe on a local Los Angeles public TV show. When Monroe's bus broke down, the band, which included Peter Rowan, David Grisman, Richard Greene, and Bill Keith, played the gig without him (*Muleskinner Live* and *Muleskinner Live: The Video*). The reception to the group's music was so positive that after performing a weeklong gig at the Ash Grove a month later, they went into the studio to record an album (*Potpourri of Bluegrass Jam*) that would have a monumental effect on the progressive bluegrass movement.

White also reunited with his brothers Roland and Eric to form a band known as both the New Kentucky Colonels and the White Brothers. The group played some small club dates; a bluegrass festival in Indian Springs, Maryland; and a tour in Holland, England, and Sweden that spring, but the reunion would soon be brought to a tragic halt. On June 15, 1973, Clarence was struck and killed by a drunk driver while loading equipment outside a club in Palmdale, California. One of the world's greatest guitarists was dead at 29. The funeral was held five days later, with Gram Parsons leading the mourners in singing "Farther Along," which White had sung on the Byrds album of the same name.

Though White's musical life spanned less than two decades, his influence on musicians has never waned. Friend and apostle Tony Rice (who first met White at the age of nine) would help lead a bluegrass guitar revolution with a style based on White's, while country rock, with guitarists doing their best to steal what they could from White's style, would become a dominant force with a Nashville crowd that had initially scorned the Byrds' attempts at country music. Live recordings of the Colonels began appearing in the early '70s on various labels (most of which are now available on either Rounder or Sierra Records), and a Clarence White cult blossomed, with initiates feverishly trading all sorts of paraphernalia and samizdat tapes.

While legions of guitarists and musicians have been influenced by White, his style remains stubbornly inimitable. Unlike other influential guitarists, whose many clones have diminished the impact of their hero's sound, listening to White today is always a revelation. While others may parrot the elements of White's playing, his was not a style that was assembled from individual parts; it grew naturally from a mind and ear that heard things a little differently.

Though he was working on a solo album at the time of his death, White never recorded an entire album under his own name, and this is telling. He was a group musician, one whose music depended on the contributions of others, and one who raised the level of excellence of everything he touched. To fully appreciate White, don't just listen to his guitar. Notice how he reacts to and influences everything that is going on around him. That way, even if you are not a guitarist or a musician, White may have the same effect on you that he has had on countless others since that day in 1944 when he first entered this world.

Billy in the Lowground

Traditional, arranged by Scott Nygaard

Clarence White's version of the traditional fiddle tune "Billy in the Lowground," recorded on the Kentucky Colonels' *Appalachian Swing*, helped define his style in relation to Doc Watson. Instead of transfering fiddle and mandolin lines to the guitar, White created a whole new sound by, among other things, combining sly syncopated runs with jazzy crosspicking. The version here is inspired by White's first run through the tune on *Appalachian Swing*.

"Billy in the Lowground" usually goes to a IV chord in the third bar of the B part, but White's first solo is harmonically the same as the A part, using an Am chord instead of an F. Over this he plays a very cool crosspicked E♭–E–A lick similar to the one used here. And the final run is typical of White, whose solos often trailed off, ending as the next soloist was beginning his solo.

Norman Blake

Norman Blake's career has taken him all over the map musically and literally. He grew up in Rising Fawn and Sulphur Springs, Georgia, and after picking up the guitar at age 11, joined the Dixie Drifters and appeared on the Tennessee Barn Dance in Knoxville, Tennessee, at the age of 16. After playing fiddle, Dobro, mandolin, and guitar in bluegrass and country dance bands throughout the South (and in Panama, where he served a stint in the army), Blake found himself in Nashville in the late '60s backing up Johnny Cash, Bob Dylan, Kris Kristofferson, and John Hartford. He participated in the groundbreaking *Will the Circle Be Unbroken* sessions and gained legendary status as a flatpicker with a series of influential solo albums in the early '70s.

Blake's recorded work with his wife Nancy, the Rising Fawn String Ensemble, Tony Rice and Doc Watson, and as a solo artist constitutes one of the most varied and fascinating collections of traditional American music extant. His recordings run the gamut of rural music—from breakdowns and waltzes played on fiddle, mandolin, guitar, cello, and banjo, to story songs and ballads whose subjects range over the width and breadth of U.S. history, culture, and geography, to blues, rags, and cakewalks performed on every imaginable stringed instrument.

Blake returned to the hills of Rising Fawn in the '70s and lives there in a three-story cabin that he and Nancy built. The house sits at the end of a long, looping gravel driveway surrounded by trees, grassy fields, a screened-in outbuilding, and an open-sided garage and workshop. Blake maintains a peaceful, rural home life minutes away from I-59, the highway that guides his motor home to gigs all over the country. He has created a haven here for himself, filled with 78-rpm records, sheet music, votive candles, gig posters, antiques, and mirrors. Wood is everywhere, from the antique furniture, unvarnished kitchen sideboards, and vast store of instruments inside, to the piles of freshly chopped logs and the porch swing outside. When I visited Blake in 1998, a roaring fire in the huge, stone fireplace suffused the house with warmth. We settled into his kitchen to talk about his passions for homegrown music and vintage guitars.

Were there particular people who influenced you when you were young?

BLAKE Yeah, there were local people, names that would mean nothing to anyone. There were kinfolk and people around this area, fiddlers and guitar players. I liked the Monroe Brothers. I wasn't influenced by Bill Monroe's recordings very much until later on, but bluegrass was not a thing that we really perceived. I remember listening to Bill on the Grand Ole Opry and always wanting to hear him, but we were not aware that it was bluegrass. It was Bill Monroe and the Blue Grass Boys, but it was just another person on the Opry that played some kind of music you could stand. I like Uncle Dave Macon, and certainly Roy Acuff has been as much of an influence as anyone in that time frame. The Blue Sky Boys, Carter Family, Bradley Kincaid. I used to hear Bradley Kincaid when he was on WSM. He had a program before the Opry show. He never did anything except play the guitar and sing folk songs. I liked Bradley very much.

I always liked all that, but I didn't care for a lot of the latter-day stuff. I liked Hank Snow real well, because he played the guitar and had a sound there, but I didn't care for some of the songsters that came on later, the modern crowd. I remember the very first Hank Williams performance that I heard on the Grand Ole Opry. Now I can go back and like that, because your tastes broaden, but I didn't like it the first time I heard it.

What about Riley Puckett or some of the old-time string bands?

BLAKE Oh yeah, I heard the Skillet Lickers on records. Everybody of any age in this neck of the woods knows who the Skillet Lickers are. And Riley Puckett is certainly an influence, as he is on many people. He's one of the real unsung heroes of the guitar world.

I can hear him in your playing.

BLAKE Certainly as far as the tone for backup guitar.

You started out playing guitar?

BLAKE I played guitar first, mandolin second, then fiddle and Dobro.

Were you playing two-finger–style guitar then?

BLAKE I started playing with a thumb and a fingerpick. I didn't play long before I started playing mandolin. Before that, I did not know that you were supposed to flatpick the guitar, or that you could hardly. And we didn't call it a flatpick. It was a straight pick. I played with a thumb and a fingerpick. I heard the Carter Family, and most of the old-time people that I'd seen played rhythm that way. Even the bluegrassers, the early ones: Carter [Stanley], Lester [Flatt], and Maybelle Carter, of course.

There was a fellow out here on Sand Mountain that played flattop guitar with a straight pick, and he was real good. He would do these kind of cross rolls. Some of my things are based on some of his stuff. There was a mandolin player that played with us that also played guitar that way, and he was pretty good at it too. So I saw those two guys and I had heard Don Reno on record doing some things. I hadn't really connected it up, though. I always kind of went back to the finger thing. I was playing the mandolin that way, though [with a flatpick]. And occasionally I might use the pick on the guitar, but it seemed like a novelty.

In the '60s I was giving some guitar lessons in Chattanooga, connected with a music store up there. And this one young lady that was taking lessons asked me had I heard this fellow named Doc Watson. And I said, "No, I never heard him." So I got one of his Vanguard albums and I loved it, but I thought to myself, "Good Lord, if this is what people like, hell, I could do this. I've been doing this off and on and nobody took it seriously." So I started taking it more seriously. That's how I really got into flatpicking.

There was a transitional period when I did both [fingerpicking and flatpicking]. In the 1960s I started playing with a lot of banjo players. I could play real strong, fast rhythm with thumb and fingerpick, so then I learned hot breaks, so to speak, single-line breaks, that way at first. I did that up until the 1970s, but I was going with the flatpick at the same time. Of course, when I started using the flatpick, everything started slowing down. Then I got out of playing with so many banjo players and it began to broaden out.

So you could play faster with your fingers?

BLAKE Oh, I could play infinitely faster. Yes, oh yes. I don't play that fast with a flatpick. I'm really quite slow. My style has gotten more arpeggiated and rolling. My flatpicking is almost like fingerpicking, I think. I think my time is really more "raggy" than it is bluegrass. I can't hardly stay with those guys. They run off and leave me in a second.

And when you heard Doc, did you figure you could just play on the guitar the fiddle tunes you were playing on mandolin and fiddle?

BLAKE Yeah, and there's other guys who would play a fiddle tune or two. But Doc was the one who was getting the notoriety. He just opened my eyes to another approach that I had already done but hadn't pursued in any active form. If I was going to play guitar, I thought you played it like Mother Maybelle or Lester Flatt or Earl Scruggs—with fingers.

When did you start writing songs?

BLAKE I tinkered around all the way back down my life with a verse or two. Poetry always interested me. I came up with a grandfather in the house who walked about spouting poetry all the time. He loved it and he recited aloud a lot. I heard it aloud and was always conscious of it from that level. And I had the good fortune to play guitar for some of the best songwriters.

People like Johnny Cash?

BLAKE Johnny Cash is one of the greats. I also worked with Kris Kristofferson and John Hartford. And I was aware of Dylan and got to be around him a little bit, and with Joan Baez and people like that. In Nashville, at that time [the '60s], there were just so many great writers that were hanging around singing their songs at this and that gathering. It was hard to sit behind people like that and not be moved by what they do. Someone said to me before I started making my own solo recordings, "You should make a record." And I thought to myself, "I will never make a record until I have something of my own that I can put forward." I'm not just a songwriter. I'm not just a guitar player. I'm not anything all the way across the board. I've kind of rolled a lot of things together.

Your songs have a lot of detail, especially the railroad songs. They paint a really vivid picture.

BLAKE Steam technology has always interested me. My father was employed by a boiler company in Chattanooga. So railroading has always been a thing with me, and I pay particular attention to that.

I always try to write some detail into any of my songs. I believe in that. If you're going to say something, you should put in as much detail as you have at your disposal. That makes it more interesting. Sometimes you don't have the knowledge of a subject so you generalize, I suppose. But if you have the details, put them in there. It doesn't make for very commercial songs—not many people want to sing about valve gears and steam gauges—but it makes for good writing.

You're also good at digging up old songs and tunes that people aren't playing. Do you find those from recordings or from people you've known?

BLAKE Oh, I've gotten them from people. A lot of them come out of childhood because I was around a lot of old musicians. I've always been very interested in older music, and I have tried to research it a little further back and see what was going on before I came into the picture. Records, books, memory, and putting it together through writing myself into it. Compilations of songs, putting different versions of songs together to make one version, including writing into traditional material. I do all that.

Do you get a lot of the fiddle tunes you play from books?

BLAKE Yeah, I have a lot of old tune books.

What are some of your favorites?

BLAKE *Ryan's Mountain Collection*—which was *Cole's* for years. It was originally *Ryan's* and now they've brought it back to its original title. I have all kinds of books, mostly of fiddle tunes. I read 'em on guitar or mandolin.

Some of your instrumentals get away from what is usually considered to be old-time music or straight fiddle tunes. Are there other influences that came in when you were writing some of those tunes?

BLAKE When I would set about to write a mandolin instrumental, I always tried to write something different, something that had some little unusual way about it. I didn't want to write something that fell right in line as to where you could predict what was going to happen. While predictable music is some of the greatest music going, I've always thought that if you're going to create something, maybe you should try to get a little unpredictable. So yes, my tunes have been purposely written with a little unpredictable twist. My songs have been that way too. When I compose, I always wanted it to be a little bit off the track, a little bit different.

The tune "Thebes" was written about a town, a little burg—it ain't much of a town—in southern Illinois. It's down on the [Mississippi] river. They call that whole country down there Little Egypt. Nancy and I used to drive down through there a lot. We'd go over to Cairo, Illinois, and go across to Cape Girardeau going to St. Louis and over that way. Thebes is nothing hardly, it's like a place with dirt streets, but Nancy and I were quite taken with that place. We almost moved down there. There's a big old courthouse sits there at Thebes. That's where Abraham Lincoln, when he was a young lawyer, tried his first law cases, and Thebes just had a feel about it that I couldn't describe. I made that tune up hanging out down there. I wanted to move down there and write mandolin tunes. That's what I thought: "If I moved down here, I could sit here in the summertime." It's just hotter than hell down there on that river, and I could sit down and write all these slow mandolin pieces in a minor key, "Thebes" being the first one. But we never did that. We came here instead.

You seem to prefer playing in small groups, or solo.

BLAKE I've hardly ever played in big groups. I like small configurations. A trio's a big group to me. I like the freedom. There's things that you can do in an old-time situation that you can't do in a group. Groups seem pretty formulaic to me as far as rhythm and things like that. I like to play off in my own little way—let things I do spawn something else. There are subtleties and all kinds of odd things you can get into by yourself that you don't do with groups. It's the bluesman approach.

You've created your career by doing what you wanted to do even though it wasn't in line with any of the prevailing trends. How have you managed to do that?

BLAKE I never felt like I was technically brilliant. I don't make records with that in mind. I try to make *real* music. I try to make music that I want to play because it means something to me, it makes me feel a certain way. If I can convey that feeling, then somebody else is going to get that message out of it. I had people tell me what's wrong with my records for years, and I think it's beside the point. If I thought that I was making records because I was the world's greatest guitar player, I'd have quit long ago. I just play what's in my heart. I think a record is just another gig, so to speak, and some days you sound better than others and some days you want to play certain things and other days you don't want to play. And when you come up on that day and there's a machine running, you play what you want to play and what you feel like you should play and play it the best you can, and you stop there. Because that's all you can do. You play the truth. When the red light comes on, I try to play the truth. And that only. When that tape actually starts rolling, you leave things out and you put things in no matter how much you rehearse it. And I believe in leaving things in. I don't believe in refining it out. I don't go to the nth degree. I like to get things on the first or second take if possible. I don't try to hone it to perfection. There is no such thing as perfection. First performance or second usually is the most real one. If you can get something you can live with in the first or second take, I believe it's better than if you go over it a dozen times.

I don't fix much in the mix. I might do something once in a while, but I really don't do too much there either. I just believe that it is what it is. I think that's what's wrong with a lot of music today. I think that what's good about the old records is that they didn't do that, they weren't so self-conscious. We're all paying too much allegiance to the great god of technical perfection these days. Those old records, they weren't worried about what somebody was really going to think about this music. They just made it. They had a chance to make it and they got in there and made it.

I remember someone once saying, "That's how that tune goes today."

BLAKE That's how it goes today. That's the way I do it. That's the gospel according to me. And you've got to put it down like that's what you mean. That has got to be the gospel according to you. When I say "truth," that's what I mean. When you go into the studio, it has to be the gospel according to you. It has to be what you think, what you feel. That's the way it goes today.

Whiskey Before Breakfast

Traditional, arranged by Scott Nygaard

Ever since Norman Blake recorded "Whiskey Before Breakfast" as a solo guitar instrumental on his 1976 Rounder album (also titled *Whiskey Before Breakfast*), this old-time fiddle tune has been a flatpicking standard. Blake also recorded it with Tony Rice on *Blake and Rice*, although on that version he plays mandolin along with Rice's guitar.

The version notated here is inspired by Blake's playing, particularly the crosspicking in measures 13–14. To imitate his distinctive style of crosspicking, approach the notes as if you're strumming through the small chord shapes, creating a sound halfway between strums and single notes.

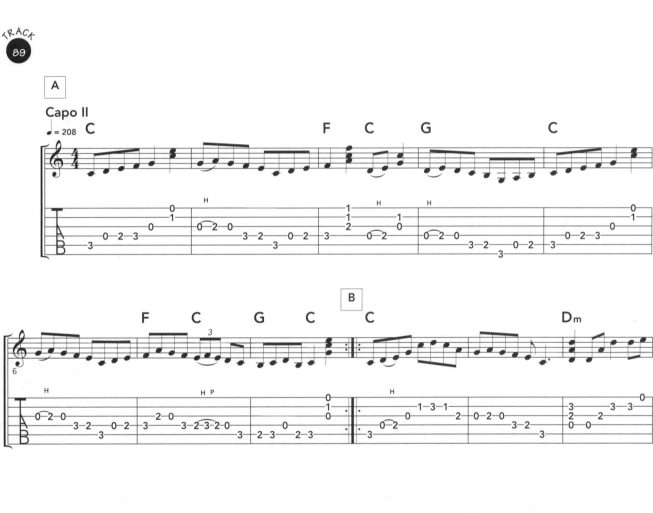

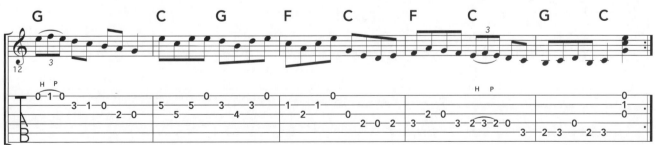

Down in the Valley to Pray

Traditional, arranged by Scott Nygaard

n Alison Krauss' version of this old spiritual, recorded for the *O Brother, Where Art Thou?* soundtrack, she changed the lyric to "Down in the river to pray" to fit the movie's baptismal scene. Doc Watson is the usual folk revival source for this tune. He recorded it on *Home Again* in 1965, and it's included on the wonderful compilation *Doc Watson: The Vanguard Years*. I recorded it on the Webster and Scott Nygaard CD *Ten Thousand Miles* (Lots of Rabbits Records, www.chriswebstermusic.com). It's standard practice in bluegrass to play either the verse or chorus as an instrumental break, but this melody fits so well on the guitar that I usually just keep going and play the whole thing. In this arrangement, I've fleshed out the basic melody with some crosspicking techniques to give it a fluid, rolling sound.

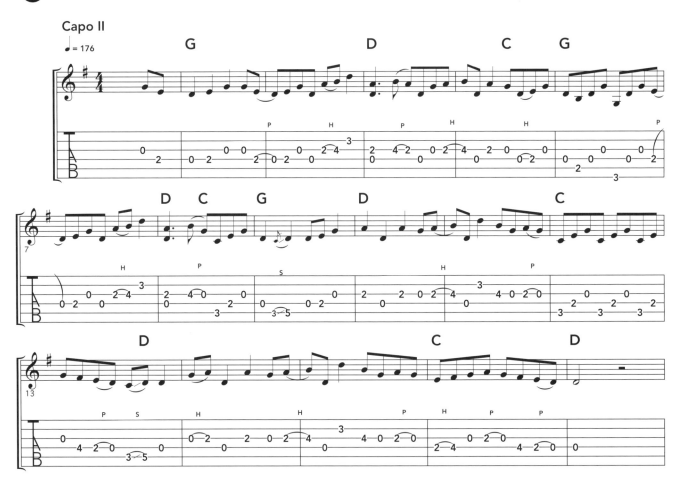

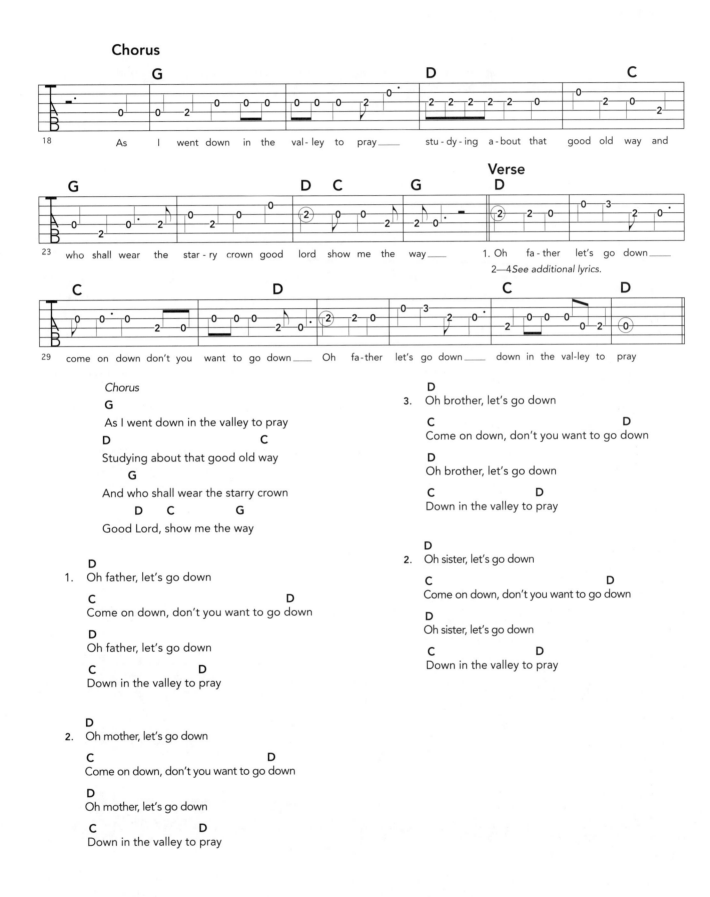

Chorus
G
As I went down in the valley to pray
D   C
Studying about that good old way
  G
And who shall wear the starry crown
        D   C   G
Good Lord, show me the way

     D
1. Oh father, let's go down
    C   D
    Come on down, don't you want to go down
    D
    Oh father, let's go down
    C   D
    Down in the valley to pray

     D
2. Oh mother, let's go down
    C   D
    Come on down, don't you want to go down
    D
    Oh mother, let's go down
    C   D
    Down in the valley to pray

        D
3. Oh brother, let's go down
    C   D
    Come on down, don't you want to go down
    D
    Oh brother, let's go down
    C   D
    Down in the valley to pray

        D
2. Oh sister, let's go down
    C   D
    Come on down, don't you want to go down
    D
    Oh sister, let's go down
    C   D
    Down in the valley to pray

Lonesome Old River
Traditional, arranged by Scott Nygaard

Aclose relative, melodically, of "Sittin' on Top of the World," this traditional gem was first recorded by Roy Acuff and his Smoky Mountain Boys in 1940 and can be heard on the Columbia/Legacy collection *Can't You Hear Me Callin'—Bluegrass: 80 Years of American Music.* The intro of this arrangement states the melody, accompanied by light strums on the top strings and some bluegrassy fills, including the Lester Flatt G run in measure 8. Make sure that the two- or three-note strums in measures 2, 4, 6, and 10 don't overwhelm the melody notes. Just brush them quietly and let the melody notes ring out strong and clear. The solo (measures 33–49) fills out the intro with a few more elaborate runs and by replacing the strummed sections with crosspicking. Make sure you stick to alternating (down-up, down-up) picking here. For example, in measure 34, play the first quarter note with a downstroke and then start the crosspicked arpeggios with a downstroke. Since these "rolls" are in groups of three, the second group will start with an upstroke (the G note on the *and* of the third beat). The crosspicking in measure 36 looks the same, but the roll is different and actually starts with a downstroke on the high G note on beat two. This means you'll play the B note on the *and* of two with an upstroke and continue alternating from there. If this seems confusing, just remember you need to start the following measure with a downstroke. The solo follows the melody pretty strictly until the last few measures, when it throws off its shackles and ends with a flashy flourish.

TRACK 91

You left me ba- by____   a year____ a - go   But I____ still____ love__ you
2—4 *See additional lyrics.*

Guitar Solo

1. You left me baby, a year ago
   But I still love you, I'm moanin' low
   Lord I'm blue and so downhearted
   That lonesome old river's my home

2. I bought you diamonds, fine clothes to wear
   Spent all my money, but you don't care
   Lord I'm blue and so downhearted
   That lonesome old river's my home

3. It's stormy weather, the sun won't shine
   If you don't love me, stay out of my mind
   Lord I'm blue and so downhearted
   That lonesome old river's my home

4. Goin' down to the river, honey don't you weep
   Gonna drown my troubles, where it's cold and deep
   Lord I'm blue and so downhearted
   That lonesome old river's my home

About The Author

Scott Nygaard is an accomplished guitarist with more than 35 years' experience. Initially influenced by Doc Watson, Clarence White, Django Reinhardt, and Riley Puckett, he spent many years wandering the sea of American music that includes bluegrass, jazz, Cajun, old-time, western swing, and rock 'n' roll and has since expanded his musical world to include traditional Brazilian, Swedish, and Irish music. He has performed and recorded with Tim O'Brien, Darol Anger, Chris Thile, Jerry Douglas, Laurie Lewis, and many others; released two solo albums, *No Hurry* and *Dreamer's Waltz* (Rounder); and been nominated for a number of Grammies for his work on other artists' CDs. He was an editor at *Acoustic Guitar* magazine for more than eight years; has written more than 100 lessons and articles for *Acoustic Guitar, Play Guitar!, Strings,* and *Guitar World Acoustic*; and has taught guitar at music workshops from Fairbanks to Finland. He is the author of the String Letter Publishing/Hal Leonard book *Fiddle Tunes and Folk Songs for Beginning Guitar* and has recorded an instructional DVD, *Bluegrass Lead Guitar*, for Stefan Grossman's Guitar Workshop.

Nygaard lives in San Francisco, California, with his wife, Anne Hamersky, and their son, Josef. He performs and records with Darol Anger's Republic of Strings, Chris Webster, the Anonymous 4, and the Scott Nygaard Band. He can be found on the Web at www.scottnygaard.com and www.myspace.com/scottnygaardguitar.

Acknowledgments

All of these lessons were originally published in *Acoustic Guitar* magazine, and I owe a debt of gratitude to all my former colleagues there: Jeffrey Pepper Rodgers, Simone Solondz, Nicole Solis, Teja Gerken, Andrew DuBrock, Derk Richardson, Dylan Schorer, Ray Larsen, and David Lusterman.

Hal Leonard Presents Guitar Instruction from

S T R I N G L E T T E R P U B L I S H I N G

ACOUSTIC GUITAR BASICS

ACCOMPANIMENT BASICS
This book and CD by the master teachers at *Acoustic Guitar* magazine will give both beginners and seasoned players the essentials of acoustic guitar accompaniment. Fingerpicking and flatpicking techniques are employed in a number of roots styles including folk, rock, blues, Celtic and bluegrass.
00695430 Book/CD Pack...$14.95

ACOUSTIC GUITAR OWNER'S MANUAL
Here at last is a complete guide to care and maintenance for everyone who owns an acoustic guitar, with chapters by today's leading guitar makers, designers, andd master restorers. Written in plain language that every player can understand, the *Owner's Manual* helps every guitarist maintain the playability and market value of his or her instruments.
00330532 Book $17.95

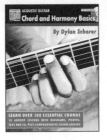

CHORD AND HARMONY BASICS
INCLUDES TAB

by Dylan Schorer
This book teaches you the real-world chord voicings, shapes and progressions used by today's top acoustic players. Not a chord encyclopedia, *Acoustic Guitar Chord and Harmony Basics* shows you what you really need to know, and offers valuable tips and tricks to help you understand and master the sounds of bluegrass, blues, folk, rock and roots music.
00695611 Book/CD Pack...$16.95

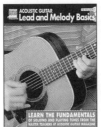

LEAD AND MELODY BASICS
INCLUDES TAB

This book introduces students to the essentials of playing melodies and leads in a number of roots styles, including folk, blues, Celtic and bluegrass. Includes a full lineup of lessons and 9 songs (including Cripple Creek • Pink Panther Theme • Arkansas Traveler) expertly played – slowly & up to tempo – by the teachers on the accompanying CD.
00695492 Book/CD Pack...$14.95

SLIDE BASICS
INCLUDES TAB

by David Hamburger
David Hamburger, leading sideman, solo performer and teacher, guides players through this complete introduction to bottleneck slide guitar playing with progressive lessons in open tunings and fingerstyle technique, tips on slide guitars and gear, technical exercises, and full songs.
00695610 Book/CD Pack...$17.95

SOLO FINGERSTYLE BASICS
INCLUDES TAB

Enrich your playing with the expressive, dynamic, symphonic textures of solo fingerstyle guitar. With the guidance of master teachers, you'll learn to build simple melodies into complete guitar arrangements, understand fingerings that will bring intimidating chords within your reach, and put you at ease with country blues, classical techniques, Celtic music, and more!
00695597 Book/CD Pack...$14.95

ACOUSTIC GUITAR ESSENTIALS

ACOUSTIC BLUES GUITAR ESSENTIALS
INCLUDES TAB

The 12 "private lessons" in this book/CD pack are full of helpful examples, licks, great songs, and excellent advice on blues flatpicking rhythm and lead, fingerpicking, and slide techniques from some of the finest teachers around, including Mike Christiansen, former *Acoustic Guitar* music editor Dylan Shorer, Stefan Grossman, and many others. The book shows all examples in both standard notation and tablature.
00699186 Book/CD Pack...$19.95

ALTERNATE TUNINGS GUITAR ESSENTIALS
INCLUDES TAB

Unlock the secrets of playing and composing in alternate tunings. Includes an introduction to alternate tunings and the players who have pioneered them (including tips from David Wilcox, David Crosby, Alex de Grassi, Duncan Sheik and more), 12 in-depth lessons in 11 tunings, 10 full songs to play, a special section on how to create your own tunings, an extensive list of 60 tunings to try – with artist songs and examples, and accessible arrangements in standard notation and tablature.
00695557 Book/CD Pack...$19.95

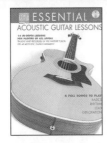

ESSENTIAL ACOUSTIC GUITAR LESSONS
INCLUDES TAB

This book/CD pack offers a superb selection of lessons and songs for the acoustic guitar, expertly played by teachers on the accompanying CD. It includes exercises, licks and 8 full songs to play, in standard notation and tablature with chord diagrams. The CD includes two versions of each song: one played slowly and the other, up to tempo.
00695802 Book/CD Pack...$19.95

FINGERSTYLE GUITAR ESSENTIALS
INCLUDES TAB

12 in-depth lessons for players of all levels, taught and recorded by the master teachers at *Acoustic Guitar* magazine. Also includes 8 full songs, including: Ashokan Farewell • If I Only Had a Brain • Satin Doll • and more.
00699145 Book/CD Pack...$19.95

FOR MORE INFORMATION, SEE YOUR LOCAL MUSIC DEALER, OR WRITE TO:

HAL•LEONARD® CORPORATION
7777 W. BLUEMOUND RD. P.O. BOX 13819 MILWAUKEE, WI 53213

FLATPICKING GUITAR ESSENTIALS
Learn bluegrass and folk featuring lessons by former *Acoustic Guitar* editor Scott Nygaard, award-winning guitarist Dix Bruce, legendary guitarist Happy Traum, and many others. Includes 16 complete songs to play: Banish Misfortune • Kentucky Waltz • Sally Goodin • Soldier's Joy • Will the Circle Be Unbroken • more.
00699174 Book/CD Pack...$19.95

SWING GUITAR ESSENTIALS
This comprehensive book/CD pack includes 5 full songs (including "Minor Swing" and "Avalon") and 10 in-depth lessons for players of all levels, taught and recorded (slowly and up to tempo) by the master teachers at *Acoustic Guitar* magazine. It introduces guitarists to swing's essential styles and pioneering players – from Eddie Lang to Count Basie's rhythm master Freddie Green to Hot Club virtuoso Django Reinhardt, and covers topics such as jazz chord basics, moveable chord forms, swing soloing, and more.
00699193 Book/CD Pack...$19.95

Prices, contents, and availability subject to change without notice.

Visit Hal Leonard Online at **www.halleonard.com**
Acoustic Guitar Central at **www.acousticguitar.com**

0506

STRING LETTER PUBLISHING

presents

THE ACOUSTIC GUITAR METHOD

BY DAVID HAMBURGER
INCLUDES CD AND TABLATURE

BOOK 1

These beginning method books use traditional American music to teach authentic techniques and songs. Now you can begin understanding, playing, and enjoying the traditions and styles of folk, blues, rock, country, jazz and more on the instrument that truly represents American music: the acoustic guitar. Working in both tablature and standard notation, you'll learn how to find notes on the fingerboard, a variety of basic chords and strums, country backup basics, waltz time, and melodies with half notes and rests. Songs: Man of Constant Sorrow • Columbus Stockade Blues • Careless Love • Get Along Home, Cindy • Sally Goodin • Ida Red • Darling Corey • Hot Corn, Cold Corn • East Virginia Blues • In the Pines • Banks of the Ohio • Scarborough Fair • Shady Grove.
00695648 Book/CD Pack $9.95

BOOK 2

Learn how to alternate the bass notes to a country backup pattern, how to connect chords with some classic bass runs, and how to play your first fingerpicking patterns. You'll find out what makes a major scale work and what blues notes do to a melody, all while learning more notes on the fingerboard and more great songs from the American roots repertoire – especially from the blues tradition. Songs include: Columbus Stockade Blues • Frankie and Johnny • The Girl I Left Behind Me • Way Downtown • and more.
00695649 Book/CD Pack $9.95

BOOK 3

Working in both tablature and standard notation, you'll continue to expand your collection of chords by learning songs in various keys as well as different kinds of picking patterns. When you're done with this method series, you'll know dozens of the tunes that form the backbone of American music and be able to play them using a variety of flatpicking and fingerpicking techniques. Book Three introduces 12 new songs from the blues, folk, country, and bluegrass traditions.
00695666 Book/CD Pack $9.95

COMPLETE EDITION

Get all three method book/CD packs in *The Acoustic Guitar Method* in one money-saving volume.
00695667 Book/CD Pack $24.95

CHORD BOOK

David Hamburger's supplementary chord book for the *Acoustic Guitar Method* is a must-have resource for guitarists who want to build their chord vocabulary! Starting with a user-friendly explanation of what chords are and how they are named, this book presents chords by key in all 12 keys, offering both open-position and closed-position voicings for each common chord type. Also includes info on barre chords, using a capo and much more.
00695722 Book (no CD) $5.95

FOR MORE INFORMATION, SEE YOUR LOCAL MUSIC DEALER, OR WRITE TO:

HAL•LEONARD® CORPORATION
7777 W. BLUEMOUND RD. P.O. BOX 13819 MILWAUKEE, WI 53213

Visit Hal Leonard Online at **www.halleonard.com**
Acoustic Guitar Central at **www.acousticguitar.com**

CHILDREN'S SONGS FOR BEGINNING GUITAR

LEARN TO PLAY 15 FAVORITE SONGS FOR KIDS
by Peter Penhallow
Add to your repertoire and reinforce your technique with this collection of 15 traditional, easy-to-play kids' songs: Frog Went A-Courtin' • Hole in the Bucket • I've Been Working on the Railroad • Joshua Fought the Battle of Jericho • My Darling Clementine • Oh! Susanna • She'll Be Comin' 'Round the Mountain • Skip to My Lou • more.
00695731 Book/CD Pack $9.95

CHRISTMAS SONGS FOR BEGINNING GUITAR

LEARN TO PLAY 15 COMPLETE HOLIDAY CLASSICS
by Peter Penhallow
Add to your repertoire with this collection of traditional, easy-to-play holiday classics. Songs: Jingle Bells • Deck the Halls • Silent Night • The First Noel • Away in a Manger • O Come All Ye Faithful • Hark! The Herald Angels Sing • It Came upon a Midnight Clear • What Child Is This? • God Rest Ye Merry, Gentlemen • Angels We Have Heard on High • and more.
00699495 Book/CD Pack $9.95

EARLY JAZZ & SWING SONGS

Add to your repertoire with this collection of early jazz and swing standards! Includes 15 songs: After You've Gone • Ballin' the Jack • Hindustan • I Ain't Got Nobody (And Nobody Cares for Me) • Limehouse Blues • Poor Butterfly • Rose Room • Saint James Infirmary • St. Louis Blues • Tain't Nobody's Biz-ness If I Do • Till the Clouds Roll By • Whispering • and more.
00695867 Book/CD Pack $9.95

FIDDLE TUNES & FOLK SONGS FOR BEGINNING GUITAR

by Scott Nygaard
Add to your repertoire and reinforce your technique with this collection of traditional, easy-to-play American roots music. 15 old-time classics: Bury Me Not on the Lone Prairie • Down in the Valley to Pray • Little Liza Jane • Man of Constant Sorrow • New River Train • Over the Waterfall • Queen of the Earth, Child of the Stars • Rain and Snow • Willow Garden • and more.
00695720 Book/CD Pack $9.95

FINGERSTYLE BLUES

by Steve James
Add to your repertoire and reinforce your technique with this collection of blues songs! Bring these songs to life by listening to the recordings on the CD, played slowly and up to tempo. Includes: Beauty and Dupree • Long John • Make Me a Pallet on the Floor • Shortenin' Bread.
00695793 Book/CD Pack $9.95

IRISH SONGS FOR GUITAR

by Danny Carnahan
This super book/CD pack teaches 15 beloved songs rich in Irish tradition and melody, arranged to be interesting and challenging for guitarists of all levels. Songs include: Black Velvet Band • The Parting Glass • The Rising of the Moon • Rosemary Fair • Whiskey in the Jar • and more.
00695776 Book/CD Pack $9.95

Prices, contents, and availability subject to change without notice.